A year in the
COUNTRY

Ca year in the
COUNTRY

Inspirational creations using
Nature's seasonal bounty

TESSA EVELEGH

HERMES
HOUSE

First published in 1999 by Hermes House

HERMES HOUSE books are available for bulk purchase for sales promotion
and for premium use. For details, write or call the sales director,
Hermes House, 27 West 20th Street, New York, NY 10011: (800) 354-9657

Hermes House is an imprint of
Anness Publishing Inc.

ISBN 1-84038-371-2

Publisher: Joanna Lorenz
Editors: Joanne Rippin and Helen Sudell
Designers: Nigel Partridge and Simon Wilder (jacket)
Photographer: Debbie Patterson, Stylist: Tessa Evelegh
Illustrations: Attic Publishing

Previously published in two separate volumes,
Summer Wildcrafts and *Winter Wildcrafts*

Printed and bound in Singapore

1 3 5 7 9 10 8 6 4 2

CONTENTS

INTRODUCING NATURE'S BOUNTY

Much of the joy of working with nature comes from making something that celebrates her beauty, rather than obscures it. The aim of this book is to retain the look and character of wild materials, rather than to fuss them with complicated techniques and methods. From spring flowers, herbs, eggs and feathers and summer seashells, pebbles and driftwood to autumn nuts, leaves, berries and fruits and winter twigs, dried flowers and seed heads, the countryside offers a multitude of natural elements to provide inspiration for decorative projects around the home.

LEFT: Glorious tangles of flower stems support the flat heads of yarrow that have been cut, bunched and hung to dry.

INTRODUCTION

Beauty is Nature's coin, must not be hoarded,
But must be current, and the good thereof
Consists in mutual and partaken bliss...
Beauty is Nature's brag, and must be shown...

JOHN MILTON (1608-74)

Let the vibrant colour and beauty in the natural world be the inspiration for wildcrafts, and there will always be room for new ideas. Each month, new materials appear for free, and although they clothe the countryside at the same time each year, they still manage to surprise, and

ABOVE: A May-time field of delicate, yellow Californian poppies in Oregon, USA.

the contrast with what has come before gives them fresh appeal. With the passing of twelve months, each fruit, flower, leaf or twig can be looked at in a completely new light, offering endless potential.

In most of us, there is a strong desire both to collect and to create, and that is what this book is all about. It is about seeing beauty in the world all around us – a lush green leaf, a delicate feather, a sculpted shell, an extrovert flower – and using it to make beautiful things for the home.

There are ideas for using flowers and plants, leaves and blossoms, eggs, feathers, fruits and nuts, berries and twigs, all of which are icons of their respective seasons. Some of the projects are simply a new twist on a flower display that can be created for a special occasion, or ways to add flair to celebration table settings. Others offer inspiration for home décor and accessories using nature's own favourite materials. Create a pretty driftwood mirror frame or an elegant oyster candle ring, aromatic pot-pourris or a love-in-a-mist obelisk – there are new ideas to try here, as well as old ideas based on traditional folk art skills.

LEFT: Bluebells and red campion in rainy woodland that is bursting with the vigour of late spring.

ABOVE: An uncommon sight in these days of intensive farming, a beautiful English meadow of daisies and poppies blazes with colour in the summer sunshine.

Spring is a time for fresh blossoms and flowers, for nests and feathers and for decorating eggs. The warm glow of summer is echoed in delicate seashells, robust fresh herbs, driftwood and the season's fabulous floral abundance. Full, ripe autumn begins with purple, green, red and orange fruits and vegetables, golden ears of corn, shiny acorns and horse chestnuts; while leaves glow in vibrant fiery shades — what man-made material could provide such variety and so broad a palette? Finally, the sheer abundance of nature as she prepares for winter sets a creative challenge. With frosty twigs, glossy holly leaves and bright red berries you don't have to be a fine artist or sculptor to make something beautiful with the natural materials around at this time of year.

The key to wildcrafts is to bear in mind their twofold nature: collecting and creating. The collecting is an important part of the creating, as it very often provides the inspiration for what is to be made. One of the most dramatic examples in this book is the Wild Barley Ring. I had intended to make dandelion orbs, but a hot spell a week before the photographs were taken meant that the dandelions had all gone to seed by the time they were needed. On our next day of photography, however, I found under the trees an abundance of rippling wild barley, soft and feathery, in that unique and delicate sheen of celadon green. What a gift! A huge armful cut with a pocket knife made no mark on the growing display, and the idea for a charming feathery ring was born.

LEFT: *Richly coloured apples are a clear sign that autumn has begun.*

Take children on a walk in the country, and you'll find it almost impossible to stop them picking up beautiful leaves. On the beach, each pebble will appear more desirable than the last. Going for a walk is all the more enjoyable when you are on the lookout for beautiful shapes and colours, and all the more fulfilling when you return laden with bounty that you can transform into something fabulous for your home.

While you are collecting in autumn and winter, though, do bear in mind that one of nature's purposes at this time of year is to provide a store pantry for wildlife, so only collect a tiny proportion of any fruit or nuts from the wild. You can always fill out arrangements with fallen leaves, orchard fruits, vegetables, corn, flowers and other cultivated produce. In deep midwinter, foliage such as fir, holly and ivy is marginally less vital to wildlife, but try to leave berries in the wild and use florist-bought berries to brighten the foliage.

As well as using fresh foliage, fruit and flowers, winter is the traditional time to use material that you have preserved in late summer and early autumn. Everlasting flowers (flowers that can be dried), wind-dried grasses

ABOVE: *Fiery shades of reds and yellows, set off by the low sun, lend autumn a vibrant glow.*

and seedheads, preserved leaves and dried fruits can be used to great effect, and the long winter nights offer plenty of time for indoor creativity. Preserved materials add a new dimension to wildcrafts as they can be used to create more permanent items such as pictures, frames, and decorated accessories. Dried and pressed leaves can become printing blocks, as can cut fruits and vegetables such as apples, pears and potatoes.

Thinking about making something with natural materials opens your eyes to their beauty, and you can have real enjoyment collecting them. But while everything in this book is inspired by

the wild, you don't have to go out into the wilderness to assemble all the materials. Fresh flowers, herbs, plants and pretty eggs can be found at the market, a wonderful selection of feathers can be bought from fishing-tackle suppliers, while you may have plenty of fresh flowers, leaves and twigs growing in your own back garden.

The key to making beautiful things sourced from nature is to refrain from fussing. Keep the designs simple and let the beauty of the natural material speak for itself. Either use all of one kind of flower, fruit or foliage, or take inspiration from the hedgerows for colour combinations that will bring an ever-changing seasonal feel to your home.

The pages of this book are intended to inspire more than to instruct and the projects themselves are very easy to do and do not require complicated skills or specialized tools. This is a snapshot of the four seasons of one year, with over one hundred and twenty wildcraft ideas put together during that time. Try them for yourself, or let them be a starting point for wildcrafts of your own, and fill your home with seasonal treats throughout the year.

RIGHT: Fruits and flowers, berries and leaves all provide abundant pickings in autumn.

WORKING WITH NATURE

The joy of working with nature is its simplicity and any techniques needed are very quickly learned. At its simplest, you can just keep a jar of seasonal branches on the table to bring a little of the outside indoors. But wildcrafts also encompass careful observation and collection, preservation, carving and drying. The next few pages show you how to acquire all these skills and equip you with the know-how to make the projects in this book.

LEFT: Gathering together an interesting variety of natural materials is the enjoyable first step for all wildcrafts.

13

HARVESTING AND GLEANING

 One of the most inspiring aspects of wildcrafts must be collecting the materials. A walk in the woods may produce some wonderful gnarled twigs or straight and slender new shoots. As well as shells, a beach walk will offer driftwood, honed into elegant smooth, weathered grey shapes by the ocean. There may be wonderfully rusted old nails, pebbles sandwashed into graceful shapes, or even, the prize of all prizes, a stone with a hole worn by the waves. Early spring is one of the best times to comb the beach for nature's treasures. The storms and violent seas of winter bring up the most bounty, and in spring there are fewer people on the beach to collect the best pieces. But as the spring turns into summer and temperatures begin to rise, you are likely to be spending more time by the sea. Even if there is more competition, there is still plenty of treasure to be found.

Search out pretty shells and pebbles, and let the children fill their buckets to bring home souvenirs of their holidays. However, do be aware that in some countries it is illegal to take any shell from the beach, even if its inhabitant has long since departed. Even shingle is seen as part of the heritage in its natural habitat. The odd pebble is unlikely to be missed, but bag-loads, taken for whatever reason, could be unlawful.

Handling wild birds' nests or eggs is also illegal in most countries. The mere touch of a human hand is enough reason for a parent to abandon the nest in some cases, endangering the survival of rare species. However, the broken shells of hatched wild birds' eggs make for fine pickings, and can be the raw material, for example, for a miniature mosaic. One of the easiest

LEFT: Pebbles that are displayed in jars of water will regain their sheen and depth of colour.

ABOVE: Always keep an eye out for pieces of driftwood on your visits to the beach.

and definitely ecologically friendly ways to create the look of wild birds' eggs is to use quails' eggs, which are stocked by some supermarkets or in specialist food shops.

Wild flowers, many of which are protected, can be another trap for the wildcrafter. You're usually safe cutting one or two stems of abundant flowers such as dandelions, buttercups or daisies, but if you want to pick a lot of wild flowers for use indoors, it is safer to buy a packet of wild flower seed and grow them yourself.

Some garden plants, such as varieties of herbs, have not altered much from their wild state. These are still grown for their flavour and perfume rather than for their appearance, and so still retain wild looks even if they are cultivated.

There are other wonderful materials that can be found in your own garden. If you soft-pruned in the autumn, early spring is the time to hard-prune some species. Buddleia is a prime example. Those long straight branches can be cut right down to within 15cm/6in of the ground in early spring, providing a harvest of twigs that can be transformed into useful containers or frames as well as delightful seasonal wreaths.

Twigs, as well as boughs and logs, can also be found in woods and forests, and woodland walks are ideal for gleaning all kinds of inspirational material. Never strip the trees of anything, though; only take what you find on the forest floor, even in summer rain and fresh winds will release leaves and twigs from the trees.

RIGHT: The long thin shoots of spring make a useful craft material. If you can't collect them in an environmentally friendly way, a good florist will be able to order them for you.

HARVESTING AND GLEANING

Little surpasses the pleasure of a walk in the woods on a sunny autumn day. So searching for natural bounty in this, the richest hunting-ground of the season, must be one of autumn's greatest pleasures. As well as the deluge of fallen leaves, nature has plenty more delights in store: bright shiny horse chestnuts,

BELOW: Ornamental maize (corn) gives colourful structure to floral arrangements, wreaths and garlands right through the winter.

sweet chestnuts concealed in spiky hedgehog-like cases, neat acorns, cones and twigs. Collecting just a little of all the natural bounty at this time of year is a task children love to help with. Give them each a bag and they'll find delight in a woodland treasure hunt.

Less wild but no less bountiful for the wild-crafter is the autumn harvest. If you'd like to make sheaves and corn dollies, which are decorative figures made by plaiting (braiding) straw, now is the time to source long-stemmed wheat and barley. This is more difficult than you may think, as most grain crops have been bred with shorter stems in recent years. The very few farmers who grow long-stemmed varieties sell them directly to craft suppliers, who in turn quickly run out of stocks.

Autumn is also the time to look for ornamental maize (corn). The different varieties come in an astounding range of colours, from yellows, golds and reds through to russets, deep tans and black. Many of these are sold ready-dried. They look best when the papery leaves surrounding the grains have been left on so that you can peel them back to give the cobs the appearance of having diaphanous wings.

Orchard fruits are another material in plentiful supply for autumnal displays. Choose from purple plums dusted with a soft bloom, apples

ABOVE: A sheaf of barley is an enduring symbol of the harvest safely gathered in. Long-stemmed varieties of grain crops like this are usually available only from craft suppliers.

in greens, russet and reds or green or golden pears. All of them have wonderful rounded forms that add structure to any arrangement. Gather up windfalls – even a single garden tree can produce generous bowlfuls.

In hop-growing regions you may be able to

ABOVE: A seasonal treat in hop-growing regions, the pretty ballerina-like flowers of hops on the bine (vine) make a perfect garland.

LEFT: Apples and safe wild fungi make glorious wildcrafting materials.

buy fresh hop bines (vines) direct from the farm. With their delicate green flowers, these really are the most glorious plants. All the more precious because the season is short, bines make a fabulous decoration for seasonal celebrations.

As autumn turns to winter, look out for fir cones in all their varieties from tiny larch cones to larger pinecones. Berries of holly, pyracantha and cotoneaster will also be putting on their best displays as winter progresses.

DECORATING EGGS

 Although eggs are traditionally seen as symbolic of Easter, their pleasing shape makes them a delightful decorative form all year round. Having said that, spring is the right time to buy the eggs of some of the more unusual domestic fowl, if they are available, such as duck and goose. See what you can find in specialist shops.

If you want to serve coloured eggs for breakfast on Easter morning, the best solution is to buy edible egg dye, which is usually available at this time of year. Alternatively, make up a strong solution of food colouring and colour the eggs that way. Although many colours can be obtained using traditional vegetable dyes, the pigments can be difficult to get hold of, and the results are variable. However, one of the easiest, effective and most reliable vegetable dyes is produced by onion skins.

ONION SKIN EGGS

Peel about four onions and reserve them for another use. Put the skins, with about six eggs, into a pan of boiling water. Add a handful of salt as a fixative. Boil the eggs for about ten

RIGHT: Onion skins lend glorious coppery tones to ordinary eggs. These have been dyed with both ordinary onions and those with red skins.

ABOVE: Use brown or red onions to dye eggs; both need plenty of salt to fix the colour.

minutes until they have taken on the colour from the onion skins, then lift them out of the water, rinse them in clear water, and place them on paper towels to drain. Finally, rub a little vegetable oil on to the shells to create a sheen.

DYEING EGGS FOR DECORATION

Dyeing eggs that are not going to be eaten allows you to choose from a wider colour range. One of the most effective ways is to use fabric dyes, which offer a glorious palette of colours. These eggs will not be suitable for eating, as the chemicals in the dye can work themselves through the porous shell into the eggs. However, they make wonderful decorative accessories for Easter, and

if they are blown to remove all their contents, they can be kept almost indefinitely. It is best to dye the eggs before blowing them as the weight of their contents keeps the egg in the dye. Hollow shells would float on the top of the solution and dye unevenly, and weighting the fragile eggs down would easily damage them.

Make up the fabric dye with boiling water according to the manufacturer's instructions. You will need to add salt – often a surprising amount, but don't scrimp, as the salt is a fixative. Pour the dye into a bowl, then lower in as many eggs as will fit into the bowl. Once the eggs have taken on the colour, lift them out with a metal spoon, rinse under clear water, then leave to drain on paper towels. Keep an eye on the

BELOW: For hygiene reasons, it is important to rinse the inside of the blown eggs thoroughly.

ABOVE: Domestic goose and duck eggs are larger alternatives to hen's eggs.

eggs while they are in the dye, lifting them out to check their progress regularly. The dye will take more quickly with the first batch of eggs than with subsequent batches.

TO BLOW EGGS

Use a large upholstery or darning needle to make a hole in each end of the egg. Carefully enlarge one hole, then, holding the egg over a bowl, blow through the small hole until all the contents of the egg have been forced out. Cover the small hole with your finger and hold the large hole under a running tap to part-fill the eggshell with water. Shake the egg to rinse it, then blow the water out. Repeat until the water is clean.

SHELLS

The unique combination of a tough resilience designed to withstand the stormiest of seas and a delicate appearance has given shells an enduring appeal for artists and craftspeople alike. Their forms can be as simple as the basic dish-shape of a mussel or clam, or as complex as the intricate spiky murex. Their colours span a wonderful palette of silvery greys and tans through to coral, pink and creamy shades.

You can use shells in many different decorative ways, by gluing them to hard surfaces with strong adhesive or sewing them on to soft furnishings in fringes.

BELOW: Clean shells thoroughly using a small kitchen knife, then soak them in a strong solution of washing-up liquid. The shells can then be left out in the garden to weather them further.

ABOVE: Drilling holes is a fiddly business, but can be done using a fine bit on an electric drill.

First, however, the shells need to be collected in an ecologically sensitive way. The best source of mussel and scallop shells is the fishmonger. After cooking and eating the shellfish, the shells will need to be thoroughly cleaned. Scrape off any debris with a sharp knife, then soak in a strong solution of washing-up liquid.

Shells can always be found on the beach, but remember that it is illegal even to remove them from the shore in some countries, and you could well find yourself facing a hefty fine if you tried to take one through customs. Craft and gift shops often sell bags of shells, many of which are labelled as ecologically collected. Another useful source of shells is to buy made-up items such as necklaces and tablemats, for cutting up

and recycling. These are often inexpensive, and the advantage is that the shells will already be drilled with tiny holes and ready to use. If you need to drill holes yourself, use an ordinary electric drill fitted with a very fine bit. To "sew" the shells, use strong and discreet nylon thread.

When securing shells with adhesive, choose one that is very strong, thick and fast-setting, such as hot glue applied with a glue gun. Most shells have very little flat surface and need to be "bedded in" to allow contact along at least some of their contours.

BELOW: It is not difficult to find shell necklaces and other inexpensive shell products in craft and gift shops specializing in items from the Far East. These are a good source for ready-drilled shells. Simply snip the thread and slip off the shells, sorting them into different kinds as you go.

PRESSING FLOWERS AND LEAVES

 A wonderful way of capturing the beauty of the growing season is to press flowers and leaves. You could buy a special flower press, but it is easy to make your own press using an artist's watercolour book and blotting paper or tissue.

Leaves are particularly suitable for pressing, since they are already flat. The most suitable flowers for pressing are those that are also fairly flat, such as primroses, pansies, hydrangea florets and buttercups. Flowers with tightly-packed petals, such as roses, are not such good candidates. If you wish to capture the beauty of multi-petalled flowers, press individual petals. This works very well with larger petalled flowers, such as Iceland poppies.

BELOW: Flat leaves make ideal pressing material and are very easy to handle.

ABOVE: Two-dimensional flowers are perfect to press.

TO PRESS FLOWERS AND LEAVES
The best time to pick flowers and leaves to be pressed is around mid-morning while they are still fresh, before the sun has had time to scorch them and after the dew has evaporated. Pick plenty, looking for an assortment of sizes. Even a single plant can offer a variety of young and more mature leaves of different sizes, and you may sometimes want to choose groups of leaves, rather than individual ones. Carefully remove

any damaged parts so that you have only the perfect-looking specimens. Lay some of the plant material on the first layer of blotting paper or soft tissue, carefully flattening each piece. If stems holding groups of leaves can be encouraged to take on a graceful curve, this will be useful. Lay another sheet of blotting paper on top of the flowers and leaves, turn over the page and repeat with the next layer.

The flowers and leaves need to be left in the press until every droplet of moisture has been absorbed. When you can lift them up and they retain the same shape without flopping at all, they are ready. Some pieces will be ready before others, but even when they are dry, it is best to leave them in the book until you use them.

BELOW: Press more material than you need so you have a choice when making up your designs.

DRYING FLOWERS

 The three-dimensional shape and, to a certain extent, the colour of some flowers can be preserved by drying. This way, a glut of summer flowers need not go to waste: use dried flowers immediately for everlasting displays or store them to use in the autumn when the nights draw in and there's more time for indoor pursuits.

Some flowers are better suited to drying than others, and one of the best ways of discovering which ones these are is to touch them while they are still growing. Those with a natural dryness will preserve well. If you become a dried flower enthusiast, it may be worth considering growing your own crop. The seeds of many varieties

BELOW: Strip off the leaves before bunching up the flowers to dry.

ABOVE: Bind flowers to be dried in elastic bands that will continue to grip the stems as they dry and shrink.

are inexpensive, and may even be sold as "Everlasting Varieties", or "Flowers for Drying". Easy to grow, the challenge is to keep up with the demands of harvesting even a small patch, as they must be picked as soon as they are ready.

TO DRY FLOWERS

The flowers should be picked around the middle of the morning on the first day they are fully open. This is important because, as they

mature, the colour dissipates and, in the case of perfumed plants, so does the aroma.

As soon as you have picked the flowers, remove all the leaves, as these don't dry well and they retain moisture, slowing the drying process. Next, gather the flowers into small bunches and secure with an elastic band, which – unlike string

FLOWERS THAT DRY EASILY

flowers from the onion family (*allium*)

artichoke and cardoon (*cynara*)

Chinese lanterns (*physalis*)

cornflower (*centaurea cyanus*)

eucalyptus

globe thistle (*echinops*)

helichrysum

hydrangea

kangaroo paw (*anigozanthos*)

love-in-a-mist (*nigella*)

bells of Ireland (*mollucella*)

cape honey flower (*protea*)

statice (*phsylliostachys*)

yarrow (*achillea*)

or twine – will tighten as the stems dry out and shrink, continuing to hold them safely. Hang up the bunches of flowers on hooks in the ceiling or high on walls, with plenty of space between each one, in a dry area where there is plenty of circulating air. The outside of the staircase is fine if you have nowhere more suitable.

RIGHT: Hang up bunches of yarrow in midsummer, before their wonderful golden plate-like blooms begin to turn brown, and their colour will be retained all through the coming winter.

23

A FEATHER DIRECTORY

 Feathers are a delightful material for creating all manner of trimmings and decorations. Soft and light, they range in size from those that are delicate and downy to the long, graceful quills that adorn the tails of some of the more showy birds. The male plumage offers the most dazzling array of colours, though the less flamboyant shades of mocha, beige, tan and whisper grey, found on many wild and domestic fowl, can often be used to create the most winsome of wild effects.

It is always easy to pick up the odd feather in the countryside, especially in areas where there are plenty of pheasant, grouse and wild duck.

BELOW: Mallard duck wing feathers show a handsome flash of iridescent blue.

Alternatively you could try breeders of fancy poultry, or local farms that rear chickens, geese and ducks on a free range basis, but by far the best are fishing-tackle suppliers, who sell a variety of feathers for fly-tying.

RIGHT: Even the downiest peacock feathers gleam with remarkable colours at their tips.

BELOW: Male pheasants' feathers offer plenty of contrast between their soft grey down and fiery orange tips, and are more versatile than larger showy quills.

ABOVE: Golden sebright bantam feathers come in a glorious tan, outlined smartly in black. The quills are a particularly useful size.

ABOVE: Teal ducks wear smart grey stripes. Their feathers have an elegant pointed tip that lends a chic finished look.

ABOVE: Guinea fowl feathers come in almost unbelievable spots, making them one of the most delightful to work with.

BELOW: The pretty shape and coffee-and-cream colouring of female mallard feathers make an attractive combination.

BELOW: The palest grey and cream topped by a strip of black and tan makes the French partridge feather one of the smartest available.

BELOW: The tiny feathers of the wild partridge come in subtle stripes of greys and tans and, although fiddly to work with, make beautiful finished pieces.

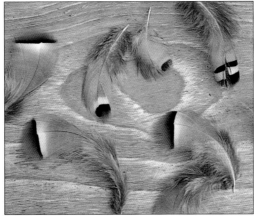

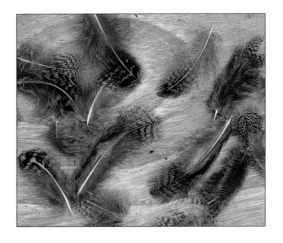

WORKING WITH FRUITS AND VEGETABLES

 The sheer abundance of fruits and vegetables in autumn makes them an obvious material for seasonal displays and decorations. The variety is enormous, ranging from huge fiery red pumpkins to tiny shiny blackberries. All add colour and structure to displays.

BELOW: Draw a pattern on the skin before carving a pumpkin, then use a lino (linoleum) cutting tool with even pressure for clear, smooth lines.

There are many ways to use fruits and vegetables as decoration. Small fruits, such as blackberries and blueberries, can be put into pretty containers which can, in turn, become part of a larger display. Medium-sized fruits, such as apples, pears, plums and small gourds, can be wired with heavy-duty florist's wire and fastened into side displays, table centres, garlands and wreaths. It is best to choose under-ripe fruits as these have the double advantage of a longer "shelf life" and firm flesh that is easy to work with. Lend brightness and a mood of celebration by rubbing them with picture framer's gilt wax, putting on enough for a subtle shine yet allowing the natural tones of the fruit to show through.

Another way to use fruits decoratively is to carve them. Apples and pears, for example, are easy to carve: all you need is a small sharp kitchen knife to make simple geometric patterns. It is safer to choose slightly under-ripe pears as it is easier to cut clean lines on hard flesh than on soft. Immediately brush a little lemon juice over the cut areas to stop them from discolouring.

Large vegetables, such as pumpkins and squash, can stand alone as decorations, especially when carved and hollowed out to hold candles. The way you carve a pumpkin or squash

ABOVE: If you want to add a touch of brightness to an autumn display, rub fruits with picture framer's gilt wax. Wire the fruits with heavy-gauge florist's wire before securing them in arrangements.

depends largely on the variety you are using and the texture of its flesh. The contents of soft-fleshed types can be scooped out completely so that patterns cut out of the shell can be illuminated by a night-light (tea-light) placed inside. Some pumpkins have such hard flesh that it's almost impossible to remove. If yours are like this, you can use woodcarving or lino (linoleum) cutting tools to carve deeply into the skin, creating dramatic patterns that do not need to be lit up.

ABOVE: Vertical stripes always look smart on pears: use the finished fruits as part of a table decoration, or cook them for dessert.

RIGHT: Available in a wide variety of shapes and colours at this time of year, pumpkins and squash offer a huge variety of ornamental forms for carving. Their hues range from fiery orange tones to cool cream and blue-green; their shapes from a traditional cushion-like Cinderella pumpkin to flat pumpkins resembling deckle-edged patty pans.

PRESERVING LEAVES IN GLYCERINE

Leaves, the icons of autumn, continue to surprise year after year as they produce an astonishing array of colour. Their transformation from deepest green to orange, bronze, yellow and red, brings with it a wonderful depth and range of tones, as different parts of each leaf turn at different rates. Colours vie on a single leaf; still-green veins are picked out. Fortunately, there are several ways to capture the leaves' beauty while they're still at their best. The easiest is simply to collect them as soon as they fall

from the trees and before they have had a chance to become soggy. Inside, they will dry naturally and curl a little, which gives them an extra dimension. You could also try preserving them in glycerine, pressing or skeletonizing them.

Foliage preserved in glycerine which is available from chemists (at drugstores), is left supple and fleshy rather than brittle and dry, though its colour is usually affected. Some varieties of leaves darken a little; others end up black, while most take on a coppery appearance. In some, the colour change becomes more apparent along

the veins. Berries, buds and even acorns can be left on sprays of leaves and they, too, will be preserved along with the foliage.

It is important to use foliage while the sap is still rising, as it needs to be able to take up (absorb) the glycerine solution that will preserve it. As the water transpires out of the leaves, the glycerine replaces water in the veins, and preserves the foliage.

Add one part glycerine to two parts very hot water, shake it well and pour the mixture into a narrow-necked vase up to a depth of about 7.5cm/3in. To prepare the foliage, remove any damaged leaves, then cut the stems at an angle immediately before you put them in the container to ensure good take-up (absorption) of the solution. The leaves should be left in the solution for about 2-3 weeks, by which time they will be preserved and ready to use.

If the leaves become brittle rather than supple, this indicates that they were too old for this method because the sap was no longer rising so they were not able to take up the solution. Don't let this deter you from having another go, simply make sure your chosen leaves are quite supple and not too dried out and you will succeed.

Left: Pressed leaves add a decorative touch to family photographs.

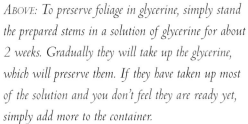

ABOVE: To preserve foliage in glycerine, simply stand the prepared stems in a solution of glycerine for about 2 weeks. Gradually they will take up the glycerine, which will preserve them. If they have taken up most of the solution and you don't feel they are ready yet, simply add more to the container.

LEFT: When the leaves are ready, they will be supple with a slightly leathery feel, and are likely to have a coppery tinge. The veins will often be picked out in a darker colour.

PRESSING LEAVES

 In autumn, glorious fiery oranges, golds and russet shades seem to invade the greens of summer, slowly displacing them in the process. So, in the mellow days of early autumn, the softened greens of late summer mingle with warmer tones all on the same leaf. The combinations can be irresistible and there's always a temptation to capture and preserve them.

Happily, leaves are just about the most suitable candidates for pressing, which is one of the easiest ways to preserve plant material. Being flat and, by autumn, a little dried out anyway, the job is partly done from the outset. Thankfully, too, they usually retain their vibrant colours during the process. Choose leaves with pretty shapes, such as sycamore, oak or maple, selecting those that are undamaged and showing the most striking colours. They should not be too dry as they will be brittle and could be damaged while being pressed, so newly fallen leaves are the best and it is a great children's game to try to catch them as they fall from the tree.

If you don't have a purpose-made flower press, place them between sheets of blotting paper and then put heavy books on top of them. A neat way to press a quantity of leaves is to place a layer of leaves between each page of an artist's watercolour book. Put some heavy books on top to keep the layers flat. Leave the weights on the leaves for several days before checking them. The leaves are ready when they are perfectly flat and completely dried out so they can retain their shape when held upright. If they are not ready, put them back under the weights for

LEFT: Autumn leaves retain their vibrant colours even when pressed.

ABOVE: The warm tones of crab apples add form and texture to autumn table displays.

a few more days. Pressed leaves are very brittle, so they'll need to be handled with care when you are working with them. They should be stored flat in a box between sheets of tissue paper until you are ready to use them. The leaves can be used to decorate the pages of photograph albums, or mounted on textured handmade papers.

SKELETONIZING LEAVES

In autumn, leaves often become naturally skeletonized as they rot down on the damp forest floor. Sometimes, all the fleshy parts of some of the leaves erode away, leaving only a delicate leaf-shaped skeleton of veins. The beauty of these has long been recognized,

BELOW: To speed up the skeletonizing process, boil the leaves in a detergent solution.

though it is rare that the whole outline of a leaf is preserved intact by this natural process. Over the years, ways have been sought to mimic the look while retaining the shape. The traditional way to make skeletonized leaves is to put the leaves in a container of rainwater for several weeks until the softer tissue begins to rot. The flesh can then be brushed away using a small brush such as a toothbrush.

Nowadays, it is easy to speed up the process. Put a cup of washing detergent into a pan of water and add the leaves. Bring the pan to the boil, then simmer for about half an hour. Take the leaves out, rinse them in cold water, then carefully brush away the tissue with a soft toothbrush to leave the filigree leaf shapes. If the end result is a little dingy, you can brighten them up by soaking the finished leaves in a weak solution of bleach, and then rinsing them thoroughly.

Skeletonized leaves look very delicate, and indeed, they don't stand rough treatment. However, they are remarkably attractive, and can be used in many ways. Rub them with picture framer's gilt wax and frame them for simple but striking wall decorations. Put them under fine tulle on a dining table to make a pretty table covering, or use them as a natural doily under petits four, fondants or chocolates on a glass

ABOVE: Skeletonized leaves look wonderful whether left natural or rubbed with a little picture framer's gilt wax, as here.

plate. Add skeletonized leaves to flower arrangements, or even use them for decoupage, gluing them to the surface of a box or piece of furniture, then varnishing over them, thin layer after thin layer, until they almost seem to be part of the original object.

WORKING WITH WINTER CITRUS

Some of the best citrus varieties do not ripen until well into the winter, so these bright, sweet-smelling fruits have long been established as one of the treats of the season. As well as being of culinary value, oranges and lemons have been used for decorative purposes since medieval

BELOW: It's easy to create intricate patterns on lemons using a cannelle knife (fine linoleum cutting tool).

times, and even now they lend a seasonal air to any arrangement. Used fresh in wreaths, garlands and table displays, they have a crisp, modern look; dried, they acquire a more traditional feel.

One of the best known and loved decorative uses for oranges is to make them into pomanders that will last the winter through. The traditional method of making these is to stud the oranges with cloves, roll them in orrisroot powder, then dry them over a period of several weeks. This takes time and can be a bit haphazard, as in the process the pomanders can become mildewed. A much quicker and more reliable method is to dry them out in an oven (preferably a fan-assisted one). When the pomanders come out, their skins retain a leathery suppleness and are not quite as hard and dark as with traditional slow drying. This method works just as well with other tight-skinned citrus, such as lemons, kumquats and the paler-skinned limes.

To dry citrus fruits, slit the skins to allow the hot air to reach the flesh and dry it out more quickly. The prepared fruits then need to be stuck kebab-style on to skewers. Rest the ends of the skewers on the edges of a deep roasting pan so the oranges are suspended and the air can circulate all around them. Place the whole ensemble in an oven pre-heated to

ABOVE: The skin of the fruit needs to be slit so that the warm air in the oven can reach into the flesh to dry it.

BELOW: Push a skewer through the orange at a point where the skin is slit so as not to spoil the design.

ABOVE: Use cloves to decorate pomanders with traditional geometric designs or simple motifs.

110°C/225°F/Gas ¼ and leave for up to 12 hours, or until the fruits are dried out.

A rather quicker and simpler way to decorate citrus fruits is to carve them. You'll need a cannelle knife (fine linoleum cutting tool), which is designed to cut fine grooves in fruits and vegetables. Choose firm fruits such as lemons that provide a good resistance against the knife, as this results in clean cuts. It is easiest to start by cutting a single spiral around the fruit or vertical lines to make stripes, before progressing to intricate designs. If you have a zester with a row of tiny holes, you could use this instead to make evenly spaced fine lines, perhaps progressing to chequer-board designs. As well as using the finished lemons for purely decorative purposes, you could cut them into quarters to use as an unusual garnish for fish dishes or desserts.

MAKING WINTER DECORATIONS LAST

Encouraging fresh decorations to last as long as possible is a priority at any time of the year. It's especially important in winter if you want the display to last through any festivities. Fortunately, a lot of evergreen material has thick stems which hold a substantial amount of water, and this, combined with the low level of evaporation in cold weather, means you're off to a good start. Cut branches of foliage such as holly and pine can last up to a couple of weeks outside, even out of water.

Most important for a lasting display is a good foundation. Start by soaking florist's foam thoroughly, then let it drain before cutting it up

BELOW: Make up a base of well-soaked florist's foam wrapped in chicken wire. Make it up in its final position to make sure you get the dimensions right.

ABOVE: Single blooms can be placed in orchid phials (vials) which can then be wired into stair swags or garlands where it is impossible to use florist's foam.

to create the base. Larger pieces will hold the water for longer, and in the case of a mantel garland, for example, you can simply cut the foam into two lengthways. Once it is cut, lay it out to make sure you are satisfied with the shape it makes, then wrap it up in a strip of chicken wire.

If you are making a door wreath, you may want smaller pieces of foam to make a smoother circle, or you may prefer to buy a ready-made wreath base from the florist. Arrange the foliage and flowers in the base, then spritz it generously using a garden or ironing spray. Once you have hung the wreath, spritz it regularly (at least every

day) to moisten the foliage and keep it from drying out. That way it should last a fortnight.

If you want to use flowers in places where you cannot use a florist's foam base (such as on a stair garland) buy some orchid phials (vials) from the florist and place a bloom in each one.

BELOW: Thick-stemmed evergreens, such as this variegated holly, will stay fresh-looking even out of water during the cold damp weather of winter.

ABOVE: To prolong the life of the display, remember to spritz it with water every day.

LEFT: A little attention every day will keep indoor displays fresh for up to 2 weeks.

SWEET EARLY SPRING

And frosts are slain and flowers begotten,
And in green underwood and cover
Blossom by blossom the spring begins.
ALGERNON CHARLES SWINBURNE (1837–1909)

ABOVE: Fruit trees are generous with their blossom, producing enough for us to share without spoiling the show left on the tree.

LEFT: Nest-building is symbolic both of spring and of new life. Create a seasonal decoration using domestic quail's eggs for a wild look.

Spring blooms and blossoms must be the most welcome of the year as they seem to burst from bare earth and burgeon from naked twigs. Every year they appear, full of enthusiasm and optimism, just as we know they will. Yet every year they surprise and thrill us with their arrival. In Germany it is traditional to cut branches of

BELOW: Diminutive speckled quail's eggs and soft pussy willow are both symbolic of early spring.

ABOVE: Pure white eggs and pear blossom make a simple seasonal display.

larch, pussy willow and catkins to decorate with wooden eggs for Easter. When they are first brought indoors, many of the branches look unpromisingly bare, but in the unfamiliar warmth they burst into life, symbolizing the annual rite of new birth.

In early spring there is an air of expectancy, even in the bare trees. There is a feeling of anticipation as the air softens and birds collect twigs for nest-building. Fruit-tree boughs brought inside not only echo this, but have a ruggedly wild look. Don't try too hard to tame

them; just settle them into large metal or stoneware containers of water to enjoy their wildness. At this time of year twigs and branches of other trees make ideal material for making more permanent items than floral displays. Some species, such as willow and dogwood, send out long, straight, pliable shoots in spring that are highly versatile for all kinds of crafts.

BELOW: Crisp greens and clear whites offer a refreshing colour scheme for the new season.

In the early months of the year, before the herbaceous perennials and annuals appear, most of the flowers have a charming simplicity. Abundant white and pink fruit blossoms dance like ballerinas in the trees, and swathes of primary-coloured early bulbs seem to be putting on an extra effort to make up for the earlier barren months of winter.

Leaves make an extra effort, too. Even evergreens, that have kept their dark green mantle throughout the winter, push out new emerald shoots, which appear like dappled light on the plants. If you cut the leaves very carefully, gleaning such treasures at this time of the year does little damage to the plant as there's a long growing season ahead: indeed, a judicious amount of trimming will simply encourage them into a bushier habit.

The succulence of the new growth allows no opportunities for pressing or drying, almost as a protest against anyone trying to harness its vigour. So gather the boughs and the flowers and simply stand them in containers, or work them into garlands and wreaths for times of celebration. Enjoy them now, while they have the freshness of new life in spring.

RIGHT: Branches of apple and pear blossom look glorious in huge stoneware and metal containers.

NEST TABLE DECORATION

In early spring, when there are still few flowers available for cutting, a nest makes a most delightful seasonal display. Tiny speckled quail's eggs, which can be bought at delicatessens or some supermarkets, lend a genuinely wild look.

MATERIALS

8 willow sticks 15cm/6in long

secateurs (pruners)

willow wreath, 15cm/6in in diameter

raffia

scissors

large plastic bag

sphagnum moss

small feathers

5 quail's eggs

1 The willow sticks make up the base of the nest, so trim them to fit across the wreath.

2 Use short lengths of raffia to tie the willow sticks to the base of the wreath.

3 Turn the "nest" right side up. Cut a circle of sheet from the plastic bag to line the nest, making it large enough to cover the bottom and go a little way up the sides too.

4 Tease out enough moss to line the nest. Looser moss has a more natural look.

5 Add a few feathers, carefully lay the quail's eggs in the nest, and finish with a few more feathers.

NOTE

It is illegal to take eggs from the wild. Only use the eggs of domesticated fowl.

DAFFODIL AND BOX DISPLAY

Using plants, rather than cut flowers, makes for wonderfully organic displays that can be used inside or out. They look just as lovely in a living or dining room as outside on a windowsill, doorstep or garden table. Here, cheerful nodding narcissi are set off by young emerald green box plants. The narcissi can be planted in the autumn and kept in a cool dark place until the shoots appear in the spring, or you can buy them in pots at a florist or market when they are in bud and ready to bloom. The display will far outlast any cut flowers. As the flowers fade, they can be replaced by later varieties of narcissi, grape hyacinths *(muscari)* or tulips. In early summer, plant the box outside in the garden.

MATERIALS
watering can
8 young box plants *(Buxus sempervirens)*
5 narcissi bulbs *(Narcissus* 'Tête-à-Tête'*)* in bud
8 small terracotta pots
compost (soil mix)
large terracotta pot
sphagnum moss

LEFT: The lime-green of the newest box leaves contrasts strikingly with the older, darker leaves, giving the impression of sun and shade.

> ### NOTE
> Potted plants need plenty of water. The compost soon dries out, especially on a dry, windy day. When the top of the compost (soil mix) feels dry to the touch, water well until the water comes out of the bottom of the pot to ensure it is wet through.

1 Water the plants well and allow them to drain for at least an hour.

2 Re-pot the young box plants in the small terracotta pots, taking care not to damage the roots. Firm in extra compost (soil mix) if needed.

3 *Re-pot the bulbs all together in the large terracotta pot, firming in extra compost if needed.*

4 *Dress the tops of the pots with moss, then arrange the small pots around the large one. Water well, and water again whenever the surface feels dry to the touch.*

43

DOGWOOD HEART

In early spring, the young burgundy shoots of dogwood are particularly prominent before the shrub produces its foliage. Mature shrubs produce a mass of branches, a few of which can easily be pruned without affecting the overall shape. Use the branches as soon as you can after cutting, while they are still full of sap and pliable, to make this charming wall decoration.

MATERIALS
generous bundle of dogwood
shoots *(Cornus alba)*
florist's wire
secateurs (pruners)
raffia

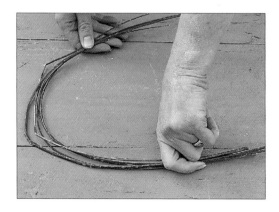

1 Select two bundles of five long shoots. Very carefully, bend each bundle into a large U-shape, easing the shoots as you go to avoid snapping them.

2 Hold the two U-shapes at right angles to each other to create a heart shape. Using the florist's wire, join the shapes together where they cross. You will need to keep easing the dogwood into position.

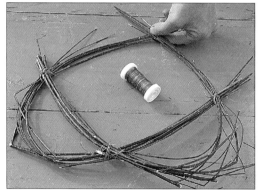

3 Wire the bottom point of the heart. Once you have established the shape of the heart, you may want to re-wire all the joints to hold them firmly in place. Trim any very long ends. You have now created the basic heart shape of the wreath.

4 Build on the basic shape, thickening it up by adding some finer and shorter shoots to the top and fixing them in place with wire. These will be more pliable than the original, larger ones.

5 Finish by binding all the joints with raffia. Make sure you cover all the wire. Finally, trim all the ends to neaten and to ensure a pretty finished shape.

FEATHER PICTURES

Feathers, simply mounted in picture frames, make original and effective decorations. The most successful compositions show a sympathy between frame and feathers, echoing their tones and keeping the proportions balanced. Most feathers look their best mounted on creamy or neutral paper – particularly handmade paper. Stick the feathers in place using the smallest dab of PVA (white) glue or high-tack craft adhesive.

Below: Gloriously fluffy and softly toned, a female mallard's feather looks delightful filling a simple beechwood frame.

Above: Quills look wonderful when not trapped behind glass, as their aerodynamic quality lends an extra dimension, with the feather tip lifting clear of the mount. The simple piece of cotton string appears to tie the feather down, while the colour of the golden sebright bantam quill is echoed on the inner edge of the frame.

Right: Neatly tailored male pheasant feathers look wonderful in ordered lines. Two large feathers with a matching pair of small ones on either side make a more interesting composition. The soft grey tones of the frame, recycled from an old barn door, are echoed in the downy part of the feathers.

SPRINGTIME WREATH

 Even a few sprigs of fruit blossom and pussy willow can be transformed into a lush seasonal wreath when teamed with the fresh new growth that brings added vigour to evergreens. The foliage here is rosemary, a profuse shrub that benefits from being cut back. Its fragrance awakens the senses, adding charm to the wreath.

MATERIALS

florist's foam ring, 20cm/8in in diameter
large bunch of young rosemary shoots
secateurs (pruners)
pussy willow (*Salix caprea*)
pear blossom

2 Push the rosemary into the foam ring, arranging it at an angle so it flows around the circle in one direction. Add the pussy willow, placing most of it at the top of the inside edge for impact.

1 Soak the florist's foam ring in water until it is completely soaked through. Cut the stems of rosemary into 15cm/6in pieces.

3 Place most of the pear blossom so that it covers the inside edge of the ring. Add a few blossoms to the outside. Fill any gaps with spare rosemary.

RIVETED LEAF NAPKIN RINGS

 Any large, leathery leaves can be quickly transformed into napkin rings. These are made from Fatsia japonica, an evergreen that puts on astounding growth in the spring, daily producing new five-fingered leaves. Riveting them together is both quick and easy, using a small riveting kit available at haberdashers.

MATERIALS
For each napkin:
Fatsia japonica leaf, or similar
secateurs (pruners)
2 rivets
riveting pliers

2 Choose half grown leaves, as they still retain their sharp green shades and are at their most pliable. Cut off the stalks of the leaves you have selected.

1 Fold each napkin into a triangle and roll the ends into the middle.

3 Wrap the leaf around the napkin. Secure in position by riveting the sides together using riveting pliers.

TWIGGY TRAY

A tray of twigs is easy to make and surprisingly robust – all for the cost of a few strands of raffia. This tray is made from young willow shoots, but any twigs will do as long as they're fairly straight and of a similar thickness. The end result is wonderfully organic – perfect for outdoor drinks or snacks.

MATERIALS
raffia

about 60 young willow (or similar) shoots,
45cm/18in long

secateurs (pruners)

1 Fold a strand of raffia in half and place the end of one willow stick in the loop. Now bring the lower piece of raffia up and the upper piece down, enclosing the stick, and place the next stick in between the two lengths of raffia.

2 Bring the lower piece up and the upper piece down again to enclose the next stick, and position the third stick. You will find that you soon develop a twisting rhythm. Continue until you have woven in 44 sticks. Weave in three more lines of raffia about 9cm/3½ in apart down the length of the sticks and one near the other end, to create a firm mat for the base.

3 Cut eight sticks to fit the short sides of the tray base. Make the first side of the tray by laying down four full-length sticks at right angles to four of the shorter sticks. Tie the middle of a strand of raffia around one of the long sticks. Place one of the short sticks at right angles on top of this and tie that in. Continue until all eight sticks are used up and tie firmly.

4 Create the other three corners in the same way until you have made up a rectangular frame that will become the sides of the tray.

5 Place the frame over the base. Feed the raffia into the side of the base at the end of one of the lines. As before, work the two ends of raffia up the side and down again, tying them together at the bottom. Repeat wherever the frame meets the ends of the woven raffia on the base, and at two intervals along the short sides.

6 *To attach the short sides, fold a piece of raffia in half and feed one end from underneath the base between two sticks, over the lowest frame stick and back down between the sticks to meet the other end of the raffia. Tie underneath. Repeat between the next two sticks, over the lower frame stick, and down again.*

7 *Tie the two ends together again tightly. Continue in this way until the full width of the frame is tied to the base at one end. Repeat at the other end to complete.*

WILLOW AND FEATHER STAR

The natural tones of willow sticks and wild bird feathers harmonize beautifully and can very easily be transformed into endless wreaths and hangings. Light and airy in appearance, this delicate-looking star is much more robust than it first appears.

MATERIALS

secateurs (pruners)

18 willow sticks, about 40cm/16in long

raffia

scissors

high-tack craft glue

about 40 female pheasant feathers

BELOW: Two raffia-tied feathers add the finishing touch to each point of the star.

1 Using secateurs (pruners), trim the sticks roughly to length. Lay three bundles of three sticks on a surface to form a triangle. Use raffia to bind the corners.

2 Repeat to make a second triangle, using the rest of the sticks. Lay one triangle on top of the other to form a star and, using the raffia, bind the star together at all the points where the triangles cross.

3 Trim the ends of the sticks close to the raffia to neaten the shape.

4 Using the high-tack glue, stick the feathers to the inner hexagon of the star, wedging them between the sticks. To finish the points of the stars, tie pairs of feathers into V-shapes using raffia, then glue them into position.

MINI ALPINE SHELL GARDEN

Create an alpine shell garden in a shell-decorated container for an unusual window box or garden decoration. The garden needs to be planted in spring after the frosts and once planted, it will grow with very little attention, producing little flowers in the summer in return for the occasional watering. It will rest in the winter, ready to grow with renewed vigour in the following spring.

MATERIALS

wooden vegetable box

lime-green emulsion (latex) paint

paintbrush

glue gun and glue sticks

12 scallop shells

large plastic bag

scissors

compost (soil mix)

selection of larger shells

selection of about 8 alpine plants such as houseleeks (*sempervivum*), sedum and saxifrage

1 Paint the box with lime-green emulsion (latex) paint and allow to dry. As this is really an indoor paint, it will weather down over the year to softer tones. Water the plants well and allow to drain.

2 Using the glue gun, attach scallop shells all around the sides of the box. Line the box with plastic cut from the bag, and make holes in it with scissors for drainage.

3 Add a generous layer of compost (soil mix) to the box, then arrange the larger shells on top.

4 Remove one of the alpines from its pot and position it in the box. The roots can be wedged under a shell and bedded well into the compost.

5 Repeat with the rest of the plants, arranging them so the different greens set each other off. Until the plants grow to fill the box, you can add a few more small shells to cover the bare earth.

DECORATIVE BLOSSOM

 The joyous sight of dainty blossom and delicate leaves bursting from twigs is hard to resist as we bring home spring's first blooms. But sometimes the twigs are slightly bare and could do with a little decorative help. Use the blossoms themselves to create an eyecatching show.

ABOVE: Soak a small square of florist's foam and place in the nest, or make a little nest from tangled moss. Push sprigs of the blossom and other material into the foam or moss nest and decorate with pussy willow.

LEFT: Use the florist's wire to fix the nest to the branches of an arrangement of twigs.

RIGHT: Where the twigs of blossom have a bare patch, fill the space by attaching small glass jars suspended from strings and filled to the brim with spare blossoms.

BELOW: Blossom can look wonderful cut short and arranged in shallow bowls. Any left-over sprigs can float gently on the top of the water.

HEARTS AND FLOWERS

 The lush abundance of ornamental cherry blossom needs no decoration or embellishment, but in a simple glass container its woody stems look charming tied and decorated with a raffia heart. This can then be complemented by more hearts, hung in the branches.

MATERIALS

garden wire

wire cutters

raffia

ornamental cherry blossom

glass vase

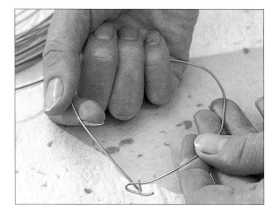

1 Cut a length of wire about 30cm/12in long, make a hook in each end and link the hooks together. Make a dip in the middle of the wire for the top of the little heart shape.

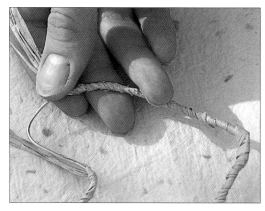

3 Take your time to bind the raffia, carefully winding it densely all around the heart, and pulling it taut as you go. Ensure that the wire is completely covered with the raffia.

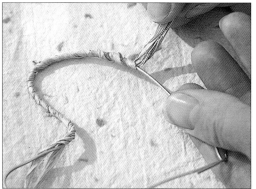

2 Starting at the dip and leaving a tail free for tying up at the end, begin to bind the wire with the raffia.

LEFT: Raffia is a natural material that is quite happy under water, and this also magnifies the heart.

4 When you get back to the top, tie the ends together firmly, then make a bow. Cut the cherry blossom branches to a length suitable for the container. Tie the branches into a bunch using raffia, then tie on the heart. Place the whole arrangement into a large vase.

QUICK SPRING DISPLAYS

The charm of spring flowers is their simplicity. Their shapes are generally uncomplicated, with straight stems and grass-like or succulent emerald-green leaves. The most pleasing way to display them is to fuss the flowers as little as possible – simply aim to find a complementary container, cut the stems to a length that flatters both flowers and container, then enjoy their natural charm. If in doubt about how long to cut the stems, a useful guide is to display them in a way that mimics the way they grow. Keep stems long and if they are branched, keep them that way. However you display them, remember to cut about 2.5cm/1in off the end of each stem just before putting them into the container to help the flowers take up the water.

LEFT: Pure white perfumed lilac teamed with fuller white pear blossom makes a lovely bouquet for a guest's bedroom. Tied with an old gold ribbon and set in a golden glass, it decorates a dressing table or bedside table delightfully, while exuding its glorious scent.

RIGHT: An old stoneware pitcher is the perfect receptacle for pussy willow, its soft tones complementing the muted grey tones of the branches. To retain the wild beauty of the willow, just cut a few branches and put them loosely in a container.

*RIGHT: Snake's-head fritillary (*Fritillaria meleagris*) must be one of the most pleasing yet unfamiliar spring flowers. Their charming nodding heads, distinctively patterned with checks, and deep green grass-like leaves are a joy to behold both outside and in. Inside they look wonderful in verdigris containers. Leave their stems long, so the flower heads can dance in a crowd, much as they would in the wild. Add a bowlful of eggs to the display for a really seasonal look.*

LATE SPRING EXUBERANCE

Here tulips bloom as they are told;
Unkempt about those hedges blows
An English unofficial rose.
RUPERT BROOKE (1887–1915)

ABOVE: Chic checked eggs are fun and easy to do, making a smart spring decoration that will look good for the rest of the year too.

LEFT: By late spring, the garden and countryside are full of the wild exuberance and colour of blooms and blossoms.

The rich abundance of late spring fulfils the promise of the early months. Flowers with waxy petals, vibrant colours and rich perfumes lend nature a youthful exuberance that is the prelude to the full maturity of summer. Now is the time for celebration. Spring festivals are a hallmark of folk cultures in every part of the world where winter bites, and to mark them, symbols of new life are traditionally incorporated into arts and crafts. Eggs have been decorated and exchanged during spring since pagan times. Abundant flowers have always been cut and brought in from the fields.

In late spring, making up a posy of bright flowers enables you to appreciate them from a different perspective. One of the most successful and effective ways of treating cut spring flowers is to use a large bunch of just one kind in a suitable container. At this time of the year, the varieties come into season in rapid succession, so use those that are most plentiful each

LEFT: Auriculas are one of the most charming late spring flowers: the Victorians celebrated them in paintings, and even displayed them in their own velvet-lined theatres. It is just as rewarding today to display them prominently in pots so you can really enjoy their exquisite colouring.

week, and you'll have a changing display with impact. By choosing flowers at the peak of their season you'll not only have plenty of material, you'll also have a less expensive bill at the florist.

Don't be too hasty to discard flowers that are going past their best. Many look beautiful in their last days, and that is part of the joy of working with natural materials. Tulips, for

BELOW: Late spring is traditionally the time to decorate eggs, the symbol of new life.

ABOVE: In folklore, lily-of-the-valley, with its delicious scent and delicate flowers, symbolizes the return of hope.

example, start off with sharp obelisk-like buds in strong colours. As they open, the shape loosens into a much more casual look, and the colours begin to soften. Towards the end of their life, they flamboyantly show their centres, and eventually the colours take on glorious muted tones. Theirs is a wonderful moving show, as they continue to grow even after they are cut. Alternatively, the sculptural quality of many

spring flowers can be used to create dazzling architectural floral displays for special celebrations. With stalks cut short and blooms densely packed, flowers take on different personalities. Displays retain their original form throughout their life, but appear to become denser as the petals open and grow.

Feathers are another delightful springtime material to work with, reminiscent of downy nest linings. They come in a glorious range of natural colours from whites and greys to beiges, browns and black, and can be used as trimmings for home decorations and to make accessories.

LEAF-STENCILLED EGGS

Eggs and new leaves are two powerful symbols of spring. Here, they have been combined in an exquisite yet easy-to-do decoration. Do not attempt to eat the eggs once decorated.

MATERIALS

cold-water fabric dye

salt

large white eggs

metal spoon

kitchen paper

all-purpose glue

leaves

stencil brush

stencil paint

newspaper

BELOW: The top coat gives a stippled finished effect.

1 Make up the dye according to the manufacturer's instructions, and add the specified amount of salt. Lower an egg into the dye. Check the egg after a few minutes, and if it has reached the colour you want, take it out with a metal spoon, rinse in cold water and allow it to drain on kitchen paper.

2 When the egg is dry, wipe it over with kitchen paper. Place a thin film of glue on the back of a leaf and smooth the leaf on to the shell.

3 Dip the tip of the stencil brush into the stencil paint and dab off the excess on newspaper or kitchen paper. The brush should be almost dry. Gently apply a thin film of paint to the egg, using a stabbing motion to give a speckled effect that allows the colour of the undercoat to show through.

4 When the paint is dry to the touch (it will dry quickly), carefully peel off the leaf. Allow the paint to dry fully before arranging the eggs in a bowl.

SPRING POSIES

 It is always lovely to give and to receive flowers, and all the more so if they're arranged in a posy tied with a pretty ribbon. The word posy originates from the sixteenth-century "poesy", another word for the poem or motto that was written on the paper wrapped around the flowers. Soon, for the very well-chaperoned

LEFT: *Blue hyacinths (constancy) and gentler-toned grape hyacinths always look wonderful against the vibrant emerald leaves of the latter.*

BELOW: *The appearance of fragrant pure white blooms of lily-of-the-valley, set against broad lime-green leaves, indicates the long-awaited warmer weather, and in the language of flowers, the return of happiness. Tied with the palest yellow ribbon striped with lime, they make a charming gift.*

ABOVE: The sharp green alchemilla leaves setting off this posy hold no particular meaning in the language of flowers, though the auriculas indicate beauty.

RIGHT: In Victorian times this delightful posy of forget-me-nots and anemones would have conveyed the sad message that a true love had been forsaken.

Victorians, the flowers themselves came to symbolize emotions and took the place of the poems, so the language of flowers developed.

With both sad and joyous emotions so easily conveyed, it is unfortunate that this fascinating language is no longer part of our culture. These pretty posies are some examples of spring messages that might have been sent and received in Victorian times.

BLUE AND WHITE EGGS

Blue and white patterns always look fresh, and this is a chic and easy decoration for eggs. The design is created by sticking on small squares of masking tape, then stippling on the colour using a stencil brush. This group of different sized eggs has been decorated with different-sized checks for variety. The width of the paper strips determines the size of the checks. Do not attempt to eat the eggs once decorated.

MATERIALS

scissors

masking tape

selection of blown white eggs

stencil brush

stencil paint

newspaper or kitchen paper

1 Cut several strips of masking tape.

2 Cut squares of masking tape from the strips and stick them to each egg in chequerboard fashion.

3 It is best to start by making a band three squares wide all around the length of the egg, leaving the narrow end free so that it will be a solid colour. Next, fill in as much of the rest of the shell around this band as possible. At the wide end you will need to adjust the size and positioning of the squares to fit, even cutting triangles if appropriate.

4 Dip the tip of the stencil brush into the paint, dab off the excess on newspaper or kitchen paper, then apply the paint to the egg using a gentle dabbing motion for a subtle stippled effect.

5 Allow the paint to dry completely, then carefully peel off the masking tape squares. Don't be rough when removing the tape as the eggs are very fragile; it would be very unfortunate if you broke one at this last stage of the project.

FEATHER CURTAIN FRINGE

Elegant translucent sheer curtains can be given a delightful trim of feathers, sewn in place with glass beads. Choose the downiest feathers you can find, teaming their tones with those of the curtains. These have been fixed to crisp, pure cotton organdie curtains. The fabric has plenty of body and hangs well at the window, providing a great base for the feathers. The feathers are sewn on behind the curtain, with a tiny glass button on top that makes both for a neat finish and adds a charming decorative touch.

MATERIALS
teal duck feathers
small glass beads
sheer curtain
needle
matching sewing thread
scissors

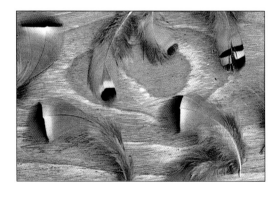

ABOVE: The light and airy teal duck feathers have a smart striped pattern that echoes the elegance of the organdie curtain.

LEFT: Teal duck feathers do give a distinctive finish to the curtain, but if you find it difficult to find them, adapt whatever is available. For example, you could use French partridge feathers such as these, or male pheasant feathers instead.

1 Allow one feather and one bead for every 5cm/2in of curtain edging. Make a knot in the thread and take a neat stitch at the back of the curtain at the bottom outside edge of the curtain.

2 Pierce the feather quill with the needle and bring the quill down the thread. Hold in position against the back of the curtain edge.

3 *Bring the needle to the front of the curtain and thread on a bead. Pass the needle through to the back again, over the feather and back up to the front, through the bead and down again.*

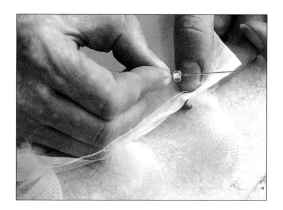

4 *Continue in this way until both bead and feather are firmly stitched to the curtain. Secure the end of the thread at the back before attaching the next feather, 5cm/2in away along the curtain edge. Repeat until the fringe is complete.*

DECOUPAGE EGGS

 The art of paper-cutting has a long tradition in Switzerland, where they use it to make greetings cards and pictures. This technique can be combined with the Victorian art of decoupage – decorating surfaces using cut-out motifs – to create enchanting decorated eggs that don't demand intricate paintbrush skills. This technique really isn't difficult, though it can be fiddly. Make sure you have some really sharp embroidery scissors. Also, use wallpaper paste as it is slow-drying and allows you to move the motifs around until you are happy with the position. Do not attempt to eat the eggs once decorated.

MATERIALS
sharp-pointed scissors
recycled paper in a selection of colours
paperclips
craft knife
cutting mat
pinking shears
blown white eggs
wallpaper paste
acrylic matt varnish
small varnish brush

RIGHT: Display the eggs in a glass jar for an orginal springtime gift.

1 Cut a piece of coloured paper to about 20 x 15cm/8 x 6in and fold it in half. Trace or photocopy the template from the back of the book, secure it to the paper with paperclips and cut round it. Cut out the wings, the eyes and between the legs. With pinking shears, cut two strips of different-coloured paper, 3mm/⅛ in wide and long enough to fit around the egg. With scissors, cut a similar strip in the first colour.

2 Make up the wallpaper paste according to the manufacturer's instructions. Using a finger, smear the surface of the egg and the back of the motifs with wallpaper paste, taking care not to let any of the paste get on to the front of the paper. Position one bird motif on each side of the egg.

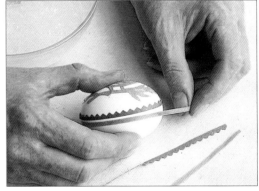

3 Smear a little wallpaper paste on the edging strips and position these lengthways around the egg between the motifs. Trim the strips to length if necessary.

4 Allow the egg to dry completely – preferably overnight – then brush on a thin coat of acrylic matt varnish. Allow to dry completely.

BELOW: These eggs also look very attractive displayed in a shallow dish.

AURICULA DISPLAY

Plant up a miniature garden in a bowl to make a delightful spring display, adding some tiny quail's eggs as a symbol of new birth. Auriculas have been used as the centrepiece of this arrangement. Their wonderful velvety flowers look as if they have been hand-painted, and deserve to be brought indoors for a while so that they can be appreciated at close quarters. Here, they are set off by cheerful, royal blue forget-me-nots. Choose vibrant colours and tiny flowers to provide a delightful contrast.

MATERIALS
watering can
6 auricula plants (Primula auricula)
10 forget-me-not plants
compost (soil mix)
large enamel bowl
sphagnum moss
6 quail's eggs

RIGHT: *Nineteenth-century enthusiasts bred auriculas in quite astounding colours, from the soft watercolour shades used in the display or burgundies like this one to unusual varieties with green and even black petals.*

1 Water the plants well and let them drain for an hour. Spread a layer of compost (soil mix) in the bottom of the bowl, then remove the auriculas from their pots and place them in the middle of the bowl. The tops of the rootballs should be about 4cm/1½ in below the rim of the bowl.

2 Next, empty out a forget-me-not plant and position it near to the edge of the bowl. Repeat with the rest of the forget-me-not plants. Carefully fill between all the plants with handfuls of compost, pressing it down well. Spread a thin layer of compost on top of the surface to make it level.

3 Dress the top of the pot with moss. Water well. Add the eggs. Water again when the surface feels dry to the touch, but do not overwater.

ABOVE: Tiny buttery-coloured violas would make a charming alternative to the auriculas.

TIP

This is a temporary display. Once the plants have finished blooming, the forget-me-nots, which are annuals, can be discarded, but if you would like forget-me-nots in the garden next year, put the container outside to allow them to self-seed. The auriculas can be planted out in the garden in moist but well-drained soil. Spread grit around the base of the plants to discourage slugs.

TULIP URN

 Tulips are fantastic flowers to work with. They have a wonderful sculptural quality and offer an endless choice of colour. These flaming red and yellow parrot tulips take on an almost architectural quality when teamed with a rusted urn. Wonderful whether it is kept inside or out, this display is easy to make, yet sufficiently striking for even the grandest occasion.

MATERIALS

florist's foam ball to fit urn
urn, about 18cm/7in diameter
large plastic bag
scissors
about 40 parrot tulips

BELOW: Parrot tulips come in wonderful rich tones, reminiscent of old Dutch paintings.

1 Thoroughly soak the florist's foam ball in water and allow to drain. Line the urn with a sheet of plastic cut from a large bag.

2 Cut the tulip stems to within about 2.5cm/1in of the flower head and arrange a line of tulips over the top of the ball. Space them so there is room for the flowers to open.

3 Fill in one side of the ball with tulips before beginning on the other. As you make successive rows, make sure that although there is room for the tulips to open, there is no florist's foam showing. The foam should hold enough water to keep the flowers fresh for several days, or even up to a week.

TIP

Making up fresh-flower topiaries uses a lot of material. Keep the costs down by using flowers that are at the peak of their season so you can avoid scrimping on the quantity. If you can't get enough blooms, aim to make a smaller topiary.

WILD BARLEY RING

 Search any patch of long grass in late spring and you'll find wild barley growing in abundance. You don't even need to be in the country – the barley used for this wreath was found on open ground in a city, growing around trees where the grass had been left unmown.

MATERIALS
about 2.4m/8ft garden wire
florist's tape
wild barley

2 Make bundles of six ears of barley, cutting the stems to about 5cm/2in, and bind with florist's tape.

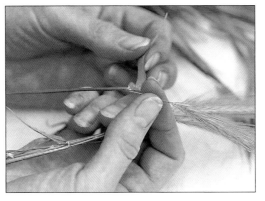

3 Bind the first bundle to the outside of the wire ring using the florist's tape. Place the next bundle on the inside of the ring, overlapping the stems of the first bundle, and bind. Place the third bundle on the outside of the wire, overlapping the second, and bind. Continue to bind the wire in this way until the ring is covered completely.

1 Make a circle about 18cm/7in in diameter, using several thicknesses of wire, and bind it all the way round with florist's tape.

FEATHER LAMPSHADES

The natural colours of wild fowl feathers beautifully complement the smartest of cream-coloured interiors. Use them to trim simple cream coolie lampshades, choosing feathers with pretty shapes and markings to complement your design. Here, feathers of similar colours are used in different ways to create very different looks.

MATERIALS

scissors

ribbon or braid

small coolie lampshade

high-tack craft glue

small male pheasant feathers

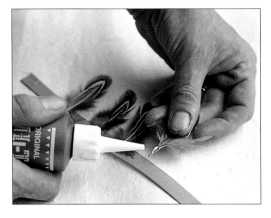

1 Cut the ribbon or braid to fit the lower circumference of the lampshade, allowing a little extra for ease, and lay it on a flat surface. Place a spot of glue on the end of a feather and position it so that the end lies in the middle of the width of the ribbon. Place the next feather about 2.5cm/1in away from the first, and repeat to the end of the ribbon.

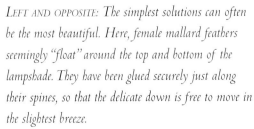

LEFT AND OPPOSITE: The simplest solutions can often be the most beautiful. Here, female mallard feathers seemingly "float" around the top and bottom of the lampshade. They have been glued securely just along their spines, so that the delicate down is free to move in the slightest breeze.

2 Run a line of glue along the length of the ribbon.

3 Fix the feathered edge of the ribbon to the bottom of the lampshade and turn the free edge to the inside of the shade. Repeat at the top of the lampshade, taking in tucks in the ribbon where necessary.

4 Finish by carefully sticking another length of ribbon to the inside of the top to neaten.

LOVE-IN-A-MIST OBELISK

This perky arrangement of love-in-a-mist would make a delightful table decoration for a wedding or engagement party. Make a huge one for the centrepiece, or several individual ones like this, setting one at each table, or if there aren't too many people, a tiny one for each guest. The lime-green of this tall, elegant painted terracotta pot perfectly complements the foliage, though blue or lilac would make good alternatives.

MATERIALS

florist's foam block
painted terracotta long Tom pot
kitchen knife
9 scabious
scissors
3 stems bupleurum
12 love-in-a-mist *(nigella)*
florist's reel wire

2 *Place the foam in the container. Arrange two lines of scabious over the top of the obelisk to quarter it. Cut off the larger flower heads of the bupleurum to make a line around the rim of the pot.*

1 *Thoroughly soak the florist's foam block and drain. Press the rim of the container down on to the foam, then cut around the indented circle with a kitchen knife. Shape the top of the foam into an obelisk.*

LEFT: *Love-in-a-mist is one of the most satisfying summer annuals, with its pretty feathery leaves and simple blue flowers. Best of all, the more you pick them the more they bloom.*

3 *Cut the love-in-a-mist stems close to the flower heads. Pass a short length of florist's reel wire through each stem and twist.*

4 *Fill the quarters between the scabious with the wired love-in-a-mist flower heads. Make sure the stem ends pierce the florist's foam, so they can take in the water and will last much longer.*

5 *Fill the spaces between the flowers with smaller heads of bupleurum to complete the arrangement and to add a little more sparkly green.*

LILAC CIRCLET

The foamy flowers of scented pure white lilac make an exquisite setting for a special dessert in late spring. Make a circlet of lilac with viburnum leaves to decorate the table, then bring in the dessert on a glass pedestal dish to stand in the centre.

MATERIALS
florist's foam ring, 20cm/8in in diameter
secateurs (pruners)
about 30 heads of white lilac
viburnum leaves

1 Thoroughly soak the foam ring and allow it to drain. Cut the lilac stems to within about 2.5cm/1in of the flowers and push into the ring.

3 Finally, add viburnum leaves to lend crisp contrast to the white of the lilac.

2 Position the larger flowers so they drape towards the outside of the ring and use smaller heads to cover the inside edge of the ring.

LEFT AND RIGHT: Sharp green and white always look fresh in spring.

MIDSUMMER'S PRIME

From bright'ning fields of ether fair disclosed,
Child of the Sun refulgent Summer comes.
JAMES THOMSON (1700–1748)

ABOVE: Fresh summer greens can be wonderful, understated and elegant. Here, a
single spiky artichoke head is offset by a jar of yarrow leaves.

LEFT: Roses are early summer's crowning glory, scrambling over
hedgerows all over the countryside.

91

The frontier between late spring and early summer is a blurred one. There is no first blossom to watch for, as in early spring, or symbols such as tulips and hyacinths, the flowers that epitomize the first warm days of the year. This seasonal transition is more subtle. By late spring, hedgerows and gardens are full of life, but gradually the flowers seem to change. The colours become softer, the petals more subtle, the greens deeper, replacing the fresh limey shades of earlier months. Then the rosebuds appear and we know summer is really on its way.

If there is an icon of summer, it is the rose. Most varieties will not flower until midsummer, but the wait is worth it. They're such eager shrubs, laden with sweetly scented blooms. Even those that produce just a single flush of flowers can provide such an abundance that there is plenty to cut and use. In fact, unless they produce pretty rosehips that you want to leave to develop for the autumn, it's a good idea to pick and deadhead, harvesting the last few blooms before the hips establish. That way, you may well be rewarded with a second show, though it will be less enthusiastic than the first.

Use roses for wreaths, garlands and candle rings; slip single flower heads into oyster shells as a pretty table decoration. Or gather scented petals as they fall, to use as an ingredient in summer pot-pourri. Early summer is the time when

LEFT: Red berries, cherries and delicate wild strawberries ripen in the early summer sun. Seasonal fruit such as this can be used as decoration and display as well as for eating. Buy or pick the fruit before it is fully ripe, pile it into your most attractive bowls lined with leaves and set on windowsills or dining room tables for a perfect scent and sight of summer.

ABOVE: Exquisite, scented roses are the glory of the garden at midsummer, and are perhaps the best-loved symbol of the season. If you have an abundance of the flowers and can pick at will, keep your arrangements simple with an abundance of the same blooms casually placed in an unfussy container. If your roses are less easily come by, choose a single stem — the most perfect you can find — and display it on its own in a tall, slender vase. This would make the perfect guest's room decoration, understated and elegant.

herbs are at their best, putting on enthusiastic fresh new growth almost daily. Herbs really benefit from cutting as, once they have been allowed to flower, the leaves take second place and diminish in size.

With their delicate flowers, herbs provide an abundant source of wild-looking plant material from your own back yard. Use them to create scented tablecentres, wreaths and garlands.

Early summer flowers are less succulent than those of spring bulbs, and this brings a whole new dimension to wildcrafts. Now is the time to begin preserving leaves and flowers by pressing them. You can use them to make pictures and decorate stationery, or incorporate them into decoupage as a lasting souvenir of this season of fresh, lush growth.

RIGHT: Flamboyant poppies are wonderful to use fresh, but do have a very limited life span once they are picked. Retain the vibrant colour and delicate, papery feel by pressing individual petals to preserve them.

FLOWER AND HERBY NAPKIN RINGS

What could be more charming than simple napkin rings made from fresh meadow herbs and flowers? Make these rings at the last minute and spray them with water to keep them fresh.

MATERIALS

FOR THE DAISY RING:

wire cutters

garden wire

florist's (stem-wrap) tape

daisies

scissors

plant spray

FOR THE HERB RING:

fennel flower head

scissors

green raffia

lavender flowers

plant spray

MAKING A DAISY RING

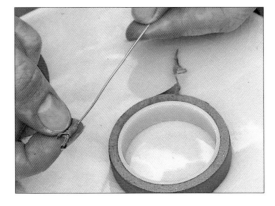

1 To make the daisy ring, cut a piece of garden wire long enough to encircle a napkin and bind the end with florist's (stem-wrap) tape. You might find it helpful to roll the napkin up and use it to measure the wire.

2 Wrap the tape around the wire, binding in flowers as you go to cover the wire completely. Bend into a ring and tape the ends together. Spritz well with water in a plant spray.

MAKING A HERB RING

1 To make the herb ring, cut the florets off the fennel head. Using the green raffia and leaving a short length free at the beginning, bind alternate lavender and fennel florets into a small garland.

2 When you are sure the garland is the right length, spritz it well with water from a plant spray, then place it around the rolled napkin and tie the two ends of the raffia together.

SCENTED CIRCLE FRUIT BOWL

A pretty and fragrant way to serve summer fruit is to make a herbal serving bowl. This one of mint, flat-leaved parsley and fennel flowers makes a sophisticated green frame for the fruit, but if you prefer something a little more showy you could add some daisies, such as feverfew, which would look charming. Herbs are inclined to wilt easily, so give them a good drink before you begin, and make up the circle at the last minute. You will need quite a lot of material to fill the ring, so the trick is to choose seasonal herbs, which will be abundant and give a lush, deliciously aromatic finished effect.

MATERIALS

florist's foam ring, 20cm/8in in diameter
scissors
large bunch of mint
large bunch of flat-leaved parsley
2 fennel flower heads
kitchen knife
plate to fit inside ring
plant spray

1 Soak the florist's foam ring until it is wet through. Snip off the ends of the herb stems and plunge them into water until you are ready. Shave off the inner edge of the foam ring to give a softer shape.

2 Set the plate in the ring. Cut the mint stems to about 15cm/6in and arrange all around the ring to create a base. Make sure the inside edge is well covered.

3 Prepare the flat-leaved parsley in the same way as the mint. Use to fill in any spaces, and generously fill the lower edge, making a "skirt" to cover the plastic base of the ring completely.

4 Cut off the fennel florets and use to add decoration. Spritz well with water before arranging fruit on the plate in the centre.

SUMMER POSIES

The abundance of early summer flowers is irresistible. Each week, there's a new crop of fresh natural beauty that always manages to surprise, even though it was with us at exactly the same time last year. It is a joy to capture some of this beauty, putting flowers into simple containers such as jugs and jars to set off the beauty of the blooms without overwhelming them. There's no need to denude the garden or hedgerow at this time of year: take just a few of the flowers that are out in profusion – they'll look wonderful indoors, where you can appreciate their beauty close up.

BELOW: Even so-called weeds from the field can look delightful if they are cut and put into a vase at home. Be careful what you pick from the hedgerows, though: many varieties are protected, and anyway, few survive long after cutting. There is no problem with this cow parsley, however, which can be picked legally, grows in profusion in the summer and lasts well in water.

ABOVE: Love-in-a-mist, or nigella, is one of the prettiest annuals, and the plants are easy to grow.

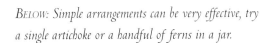

BELOW: Simple arrangements can be very effective, try a single artichoke or a handful of ferns in a jar.

RIGHT: Roses always look romantic and it's no wonder that they have inspired poets for centuries. They are generous with their blooms and should be enjoyed indoors too. Older shrubs offer up armfuls of flowers without affecting the show in the garden.

SHELL BASKET

The smooth shiny surface of cowrie shells is a beautiful foil for the rugged texture of basketwork. A simple and inexpensive basket from the Far East can be given an exotic look with a pretty fringe of cowries, and used to store anything from onions and garlic in the kitchen to linens, handkerchiefs or even sewing theads. Alternatively, use it as a wonderful container for an unpretentious dried flower arrangement, or use it as somewhere to display the shells and pebbles you collected from the beach when you were last on holiday.

MATERIALS
needle

nylon thread

scissors

natural raffia

cowrie shells drilled at both ends

basket

glue gun and glue sticks

TIP
The shells need to have holes drilled with a fine bit before threading, unless you can find them with ready-made holes: these were cut from an inexpensive shell mat.

1 Thread a needle with nylon thread and knot the two ends together. Cut a piece of raffia about 5cm/2in long and bring the nylon thread around its centre, passing the needle back between the knotted threads. Pull tight so the raffia is now firmly held at the end of the thread. Pass the needle through the hole at one end of a cowrie shell.

2 Bring the needle up through the hole at the other end. Repeat with four more shells, to make a string of five.

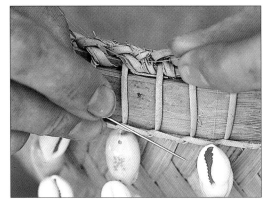

3 Sew the shells firmly to the rim of the basket, taking the thread to the inside to secure it. Cut the thread and repeat the process until you have completed the fringing.

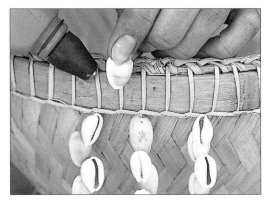

4 Using the glue gun, stick a border of single cowrie shells around the rim of the basket to complete the decoration. Make sure you have enough shells before you begin to do this, and plan how close they can be.

LEAF PICTURES

Leaves make charming pictures, and can be used to create endless different effects. They need to be pressed first, to thoroughly preserve them. There's no need to be too ambitious: show off the beauty of the leaves at their best by selecting pretty shapes and displaying them simply in a frame. Don't be tempted to use adhesives, which can be messy. Simply lay the leaves on the glass, add a backing sheet and re-assemble the frame.

ABOVE: Yarrow (achillea) leaves have a wonderful feathery quality, and they grow in profusion. Press lots of leaves so you have plenty of choice when making up the arrangement. These leaves have been mounted on a piece of Mexican bark paper, but any creamy textured paper background will do.

LEFT: Wisteria leaves look quite different when displayed in isolation. Make use of the graceful curves of their stems and mount them cropped close in a beechwood frame.

BELOW: If you can find or construct a frame with two pieces of glass, this can be a wonderful way to display prettily shaped leaves such as maple. Just choose one beautiful specimen and show it off in all its glory, so it appears to float in the frame.

RIGHT: Simple leaf pictures can look highly effective when grouped together. The key is to make uncluttered arrangements of the leaves, taking your inspiration from old botanical prints. That way, they complement rather than compete with each other.

WILD GARLAND

Wild-looking flowers make the prettiest table garlands for summer celebration meals. Garlands do use a lot of material, so it's better not to rely on the countryside. If you don't have enough suitable flowers in the garden, look in the florist for cultivated versions.

MATERIALS
FOR ABOUT 1M/3FT GARLAND
2 blocks florist's foam
kitchen knife
garland cradles or chicken wire (see Tip)
secateurs (pruners)
2 large bunches of dill
2 bunches of bupleurum
2 bunches of knapweed (Centaurea montana)
plant spray

TIP
If you can't get garland cradles, make the support for the garland from chicken wire. Cut a rectangle of chicken wire to the desired length of the finished garland and about 20cm/8in wide. Cut the foam into blocks about 5cm/2in wide and deep and lay these along the chicken wire, then roll up into a sausage.

1 Thoroughly soak the florist's foam in water, then cut it up into blocks to fit the garland cradles. Cut the dill stems to about 2.5cm/1in and position in the foam to create a base.

2 Cut off the individual heads of the bupleurum and add them all along the garland for texture.

3 Finally, decorate the garland with the knapweed heads for some added colour. Thoroughly spritz with water using a plant spray.

LEFT: Frothy white dill, green bupleurum and pretty purple knapweed (Centaurea montana) make a wonderful wild-looking garland.

ROSE CANDLE RING

A candle ring of garden roses, set in a footed bowl, makes a most delightful summer tablecentre. The roses don't have to be all the same variety – a mixture looks charming – so there is no need to denude one shrub. Adding in a few rosehips lends a little structure to the arrangement and gives a slightly wilder look.

MATERIALS
florist's foam ball
kitchen knife
footed glass bowl
candle
secateurs (pruners)
selection of garden roses, including hips

1 Thoroughly soak the florist's foam ball in water – this should take at least half an hour. Cut in half.

2 Place one of the soaked half-balls in the bowl and push the candle into the middle.

LEFT: *Pick full-blown roses from the garden – the delicate yellow stamens in the centres add extra appeal.*

3 Cut the rose stems to a length of about 2.5cm/1in. Arrange the roses to cover the foam base completely.

4 Add a few leaves and bunches of rosehips to complete the candle ring and give it a wilder, less contrived personality.

SUMMER POT-POURRI

 Capture the scent of summer by making your own pot-pourri. Lavender provides a wonderful aromatic base and retains its scent for many months. Roses can be another ingredient from the garden, supplemented if necessary with bought dried petals. The perfumes will then need to be enhanced by essential oils and fixed with orris root to make a glorious reminder of summer that will last right into the winter.

MATERIALS

6ml/120 drops lavender essential oil

5ml/100 drops geranium essential oil

small bottle

25g/1oz ground orris root

15g/½ oz whole cloves

15g/½ oz dried mace

115g/4oz dried lavender

225g/8oz dried rose petals

225g/8oz dried rosebuds

mixing bowl

wooden spoon

RIGHT: Deep purple lavender and delicate pink garden roses go together perfectly, and make a fragrant and pretty base for summer pot-pourri.

1 First make up a blend of the essential oils in a small bottle and shake well. Add a little of this to the ground orris root and stir to create a crumbly mixture.

2 Add the rest of the blended oil to the dried spices and mix well. Cover and leave in a dark place for 24 hours to allow the fragrances to mingle.

3 Gather together the dried petals and flowers, then mix them together in a large bowl using a wooden spoon. Add the dried spices, now well scented by the blended oils, and mix these in well. Add the orris root mixture, and stir well again. Cover and leave in a dark place for up to 6 weeks.

MEXICAN BARK FOLDER

The subtle natural tones of Mexican bark paper, driftwood and raffia combine beautifully to make exquisite gift stationery. Fill this lovely folder with toning paper and envelopes to make a present that would delight anyone, of any age, for any occasion.

MATERIALS
paper and pencil for template
scissors
Mexican bark paper or other firm paper
natural raffia
small piece of driftwood
craft glue
darning needle

1 Copy the template from the back of the book, scale it up to a size to fit your stationery, and cut it out. Cut out the shape in Mexican bark paper. Cut four small squares from the remaining bark paper. Cut a length of raffia and wrap it around the driftwood, tying it firmly. Add a spot of glue underneath to secure. Mark the spot on the front of the folder where the driftwood toggle is to go. Thread the needle with a strand of raffia and pass the needle through one small paper square, then through the marked spot, from the back.

2 Thread a second small paper square on to the needle, then pass the needle through the raffia band on the driftwood and back again to the back. Knot the two ends of the raffia securely at the back and trim.

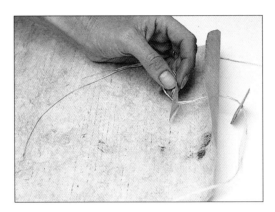

3 Mark the position for the raffia loop on the flap of the folder, aligning it with the toggle. Place the four paper squares in position, pass the needle from the back of the folder, then, leaving a loop, pass it back through the same hole.

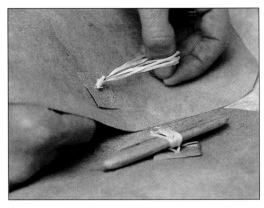

4 You will need to make a knot at the base of the loop. Gauge the position of this by trying the loop over the driftwood, allowing a little extra length for the knot. Make the knot, try the loop over the toggle again and adjust if necessary. At the back of the flap, tie another knot to secure the loop. Trim the ends of the raffia.

5 Turn in the side flaps and glue the front of the pocket in position. Leave to dry before filling the folder with some appropriate stationery.

SUMMER WREATH

 The unlikely combination of wild cow parsley and pale pink garden roses makes an incredibly pretty wreath. The frothy texture of the cow parsley makes an exquisite contrast with the creamy-smooth petals of the roses.

MATERIALS
florist's foam ring
garden and wild roses
large bunch of cow parsley
secateurs (pruners)

2 Continue to add roses until you are happy with the arrangement. Add rosebuds, rosehips and leaves if you want a wilder look. Fill in with the cow parsley for a pretty finished effect, covering the foam ring completely.

1 Immerse the florist's foam ring in water for up to half an hour, until thoroughly soaked. Gather together the plant material. Start by positioning the roses, first cutting the stems to about 2.5cm/1in.

3 Finally, add a few single or wild roses, taking care that they are not swamped by the other flowers. Give the wreath a good spritz with water.

HIGH SUMMER

Fair flowers that are not gather'd in their prime,
Rot and consume themselves in little time.
William Shakespeare (1564-1616)

ABOVE: *Shells from the beach make beautiful decorative pieces all by themselves, and will also remind you of your summer holiday.*

LEFT: *Late summer flowers have mellower hues than early summer blooms, and many, like lavender, carry scented oils to protect them from drying out in the heat.*

115

The sheer variety of flowers and leaves in summer is astonishing. As the season progresses, it seems there is no end to new arrivals, and then, as the days get hotter, the countryside takes on a much drier look. Many late summer flowers have small, papery petals, and some almost dry on the stem. Think of lavender, yarrow, statice, thistles or alliums, those fabulous globe-like flowers produced by the onion family.

ABOVE: Gloriously architectural, artichoke heads look wonderful simply standing in a large glass jar.

LEFT: Place a single head of cow parsley in a small glass jug as an instant and pretty table decoration for a summer afternoon.

Late summer is one of the best times of the year to collect material that can be preserved: while in early summer you can begin to press plant material, late summer is the time of year to harvest and dry flowers and leaves that can be used immediately, or stored, ready for use during the longer autumn nights.

Dried material that you plan to keep should be stored carefully as it is very brittle. The best plan is to hang it upside down in a well-ventilated room where it won't be knocked. Alternatively, store it, well protected with plenty of paper tissue, in roomy boxes in a cool, dry place. That way it should last well into winter.

Hotter days take us outside: on trips to the beach and the river bank, both rich sources of material that can be used to make all manner of things. Even the smallest pieces of driftwood can be put to good use, and shells always have a place in the repertoire of wildcrafts. Give children a bucket each, and they will enjoy seeking out pretty pebbles and shells, as well as unusual pieces of driftwood.

If the call of the great outdoors precludes much in the way of creativity, use this as a time to build up a bank of material for future use when the nights draw in. However, there are some things, such as lavender and eucalyptus wreaths, that are best made while the material is still fresh and pliable. Once completed, they can be allowed to dry, providing decoration right through the winter.

RIGHT: Thistles and driftwood, shells and leaves are just a small part of the rich supply of materials offered by nature in the summer months.

OYSTER CANDLE RING

Oyster shells make the prettiest candleholders, and are easy to get hold of from most fishmongers. With a nightlight (tealight), scented if possible, in each one, they become charming low-level lights for the table. Here, several have been arranged in a circle with other shells filled with water to hold roses.

MATERIALS

12 oyster shells
6 nightlights (tealights)
scissors
6 roses

1 Arrange the oyster shells in a circle, some rugged side up. Place a nightlight (tealight) in six of the shells.

2 Fill some of the remaining shells with water. Cut the rose stems very short and arrange in the shells.

ABOVE: The rugged layered and fluted undersides of oyster shells make a fabulous contrast with the glossy, luxurious mother-of-pearl insides. Arrange the shells so that insides and outsides both show.

ABOVE: Oyster-shell candles make pretty table lights that are far below eye level, and so will never dazzle. Don't leave them burning unattended.

LEFT: Delicate pinky-cream rose petals look perfectly wonderful set against the rugged undersides of mature oyster shells.

THISTLE POT

Thistles dry easily and their textural quality makes for glorious everlasting arrangements. Late summer is the time to pick or buy thistles – look for those that have a dense, feathery appearance. Here *eryngium* (sea holly) has been used.

MATERIALS
2 blocks of florist's dry foam
kitchen knife and board
florist's reel wire
container about 15cm/6in wide
washing-up or garden gloves
about 100 heads of large thistles
secateurs (pruners)

2 Using the kitchen knife, cut off the bottom of the florist's foam so that it fits into the container. Check for size and trim if necessary.

4 Put on the washing-up gloves to protect your fingers. Cut the thistle stems to about 2.5cm/1in and begin by fixing in the bottom row.

1 Place the blocks of foam on the board side by side and wire them together using a piece of reel wire.

3 Trim off the top corners of the foam block to create an obelisk shape, then fit the block into the container.

5 Continue to fix in the thistles so that they cover the whole of the obelisk.

EUCALYPTUS WREATH

 Eucalyptus is a fabulous foliage. Robust yet not rigid, it falls prettily and its wonderful bluey-green shades are most sympathetic to many colour schemes. There are many varieties: the young leaves may be round or oval, like those used here. The foliage of mature trees is much longer and more feathery. Once made, this wreath can be hung up and will dry naturally.

MATERIALS
garden wire

florist's (stem-wrap) tape

heavy gauge florist's reel wire

large bunch of eucalyptus

2 Using reel wire, attach a small branch of eucalyptus to the ring. Wire the other end of the stem to the ring. Add another branch of eucalyptus, again wiring it at the top and bottom.

1 Using three thicknesses of garden wire, make a circle about 36cm/14in in diameter and bind with florist's (stem-wrap) tape.

3 Add extra branches to fill out the wreath. Continue in this way all around the wire ring until the wreath is complete and looks rich and lush.

SHELL FISH WALL HANGING

This witty fishy wall hanging is deceptively easy to make, and the overall effect is reminiscent of a Victorian shell grotto. The trick when working with shells is to keep the design simple, and use them to suggest relevant textures. Here, the rhythmic arrangement of the mussel shells mimics scales, while small cowries are used for a finer-textured nose and spiral-shaped augers naturally fan out for the tail.

MATERIALS

paper for template

scissors

sheet of 1mm/³/100in plywood, at least 50 x 18cm/20 x 7in (available from model shops)

soft pencil

fine jigsaw or heavy-duty craft knife

quick drying primer

paintbrush

grey-green emulsion (latex) paint

glue gun and glue sticks

small sundial shell or similar

small cowrie shells

mussel shells

5 augur shells

a few tiny shells

1 *Enlarge the fish template from the back of the book to a length of about 50cm/20in. Cut out. Place the template on the plywood and draw around it and cut out the fish shape using a jigsaw or a heavy-duty craft knife. Brush on primer and allow to dry. Paint with a coat of grey-green emulsion (latex) and leave to dry.*

2 *Stick on the shells using a glue gun. Start by positioning the eye, then arrange the cowries for the nose and head.*

3 *Arrange the mussel shells in rows, sticking on the first row with the flat edge up; the next with the flat edge down. Where necessary, to retain the curved shape of the fish, you may have to turn some shells the other way at the edges. Try out each row to check that it fits before you start to glue it.*

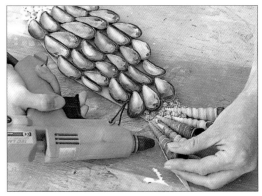

4 *Arrange and glue the augurs for the tail, letting them fan out with the wide ends at the tail, then fill in with tiny shells around the points of the augurs.*

QUICK WAYS WITH LAVENDER

 The heady, slightly medicinal aroma of lavender, redolent of summer, is hard to resist at any time of the year. It retains its inimitable fragrance even when dried, and can be used to scent rooms and linens deep into the winter. Lavender dries readily both on and off the stalk, and when cut bunches are dried, they retain their wonderfully sculptural shape, though the deep purple tones tend to soften. This makes lavender an ideal flower for dried arrangements and wreaths.

LEFT: The intense tones of lavender look even richer when teamed with similar tones. Here, lavender has simply been put into old-fashioned sugar bags that complement it perfectly.

BELOW: Freshly picked lavender looks glorious just put unceremoniously in the simplest of bowls.

LEFT: Open bowls of dried lavender tend to attract dust. Taking inspiration from traditional pomanders, which have holes through which the scent is released, here the lavender is put in an old sugar shaker.

RIGHT: Lavender bags can be the simplest of affairs. Here, dried flowers have been tied up in an old teacloth to use to freshen and scent the linen cupboard.

FRESH LAVENDER TUSSIE MUSSIE

In bygone days, ladies carried herbal tussie mussies as a form of personal perfume. They were usually made of several varieties of fresh herbs arranged in concentric circles. If you are lucky enough to find white lavender, or if you grow it in your own garden, it will look great in a delightful tussie mussie when contrasted with the more conventional blue.

MATERIALS
I bunch blue lavender
I bunch white lavender
green raffia, similar twine or rubber band
pruning shears
ribbon

1 Arrange a circle of deep blue lavender stems around a small bunch of the white lavender. Secure with a piece of raffia, twine or a rubber band.

2 Arrange the remaining white stalks of lavender around the blue, and secure the complete bunch with raffia, twine or a rubber band. Trim the stalks to an even length using pruning shears.

3 Complete the arrangement by tying on a wide ribbon, then making a generous, decorative bow.

FEATHERY ORGANDIE CLOTH

The delightful spotty guinea fowl feathers perfectly complement the delicate organdie tablecloth. The feathers are easy to remove from their pockets for washing. Buy plenty of them so you can select at least 24 of a similar size.

MATERIALS
scissors

1.1m/1¼ yd white cotton organdie, 120cm/48in wide

needle

white sewing thread

white tulle, about 100 x 10cm/40 x 4in

pins

white stranded embroidery thread (floss)

24 guinea fowl feathers

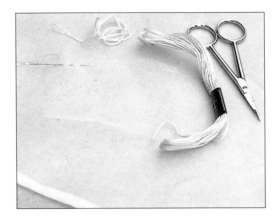

2 Cut the tulle into 12 rectangles, about 7.5 x 5cm/3 x 2in. Pin the pockets on to the cloth, arranging four in a diagonal line from corner to corner, then a parallel row of three on either side, and one near each of the remaining corners. With two strands of embroidery thread (floss), stitch each pocket into position, leaving one short side open.

4 For each corner, cut a strip about 22 x 2.5cm/ 9 x 1in from the remaining organdie. Fold each strip in half lengthways, turn in the sides and ends and slipstitch all around to make a tie. Make a bunch of three similar-sized feathers and stitch them to the middle of the tie. Tie the tie in a single knot around the bunch of feathers.

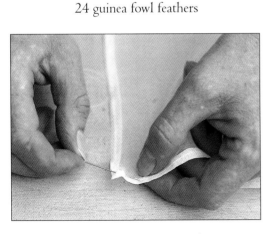

1 Trim the organdie to make a 110cm/43in square. Turn in and stitch a double hem around all four sides.

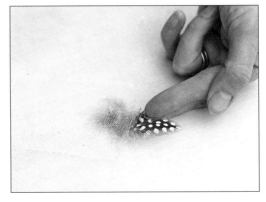

3 Select 12 similar-sized guinea fowl feathers, and slip one into each pocket, quill end first.

5 Neatly stitch a tied feather trim to each corner of the tablecloth.

HEART OF GOLD

Yarrow *(achillea)* is one of the most satisfying flowers to dry. It's an easy-to-grow perennial, and the glorious golden plate-like blooms begin to dry almost as soon as they open. Enjoy them in the garden for a few weeks, then cut them before they start to go brown. Strip off the leaves and hang them upside down in a dry, airy place, and in a week or so they'll be ready to use. These dense-headed blooms make wonderful dried flowers for providing solid colour, as on this charming golden heart.

MATERIALS
2 blocks of florist's dry foam
scissors
newspaper
pencil
kitchen knife
heavy gauge florist's reel wire
large bunch of yarrow
natural raffia

1 Lay the foam blocks side by side and cut a piece of newspaper to this dimension. Fold it in half and draw half a heart shape with the dip and the point at the fold. Cut out the template, unfold it and lay it on the foam, then cut around it using a kitchen knife.

2 Turn each heart shape on its side and cut in half so it is not so deep and bulky.

3 Use florist's reel wire to bind the two halves of the heart together. Cut the florets off the yarrow and push them into the foam until the top of the heart shape is completely covered.

4 Make a bundle of raffia thick enough to cover the side of the florist's foam base, fold it in half to find the middle and wind a piece of florist's reel wire around it. Twist the ends together. Push this wire into the top dip in the heart.

5 Take the raffia to the point of the heart and tie the ends together in a neat reef knot. Trim the ends. Finally, add extra florets of yarrow to cover any bare areas of the florist's foam base.

DRIFTWOOD MIRROR

 The muted, weathered tones and contorted shapes of driftwood just beg to be used. Here, a shabby old mirror frame has been transformed using the curved edge of an old garden table for the top and various pieces of driftwood to make a wonderful organic decoration.

MATERIALS
driftwood of various sizes
old mirror in a wooden frame
screws
screwdriver
hammer
nails

2 Screw the main pieces of driftwood to the frame to ensure they are really secure.

3 Add small decorative pieces of driftwood to the frame using a hammer and small nails, making an attractive design as you go.

1 Move the pieces around to create a design for the frame. If you need to widen a piece, simply screw on an extra section as here.

LAVENDER CUSHION

Lavender may be associated with a bygone age, but that does not mean it has to stay in the past. This cushion is up-to-date, yet still exudes that glorious fragrance. The inner sachet means you can wash the cover and replace the lavender.

MATERIALS

natural linen, 23 x 45cm/9 x 18in
matching sewing thread
sewing machine
blue linen, 23 x 45cm/9 x 18in
6 small metal buttons
6 snap fasteners
voile, 30 x 45cm/12 x 18in
130gm/4½oz dried lavender

1 Fold over and stitch a double hem along one long side of the natural linen. With right sides together, stitch the other long side to one long side of the blue linen.

2 Press the seam allowance towards the blue linen, then sew a double row of topstitching on the blue side.

3 With right sides together, fold the whole piece in half and stitch the long side and the short blue side. Snip the corners and turn through.

4 Fold half of the natural linen section to the inside. Sew a double row of topstitching around three sides of the cover, leaving the natural side open. Stitch the buttons in place down the centre of the natural panel, stitching snap fasteners behind them to close the cover.

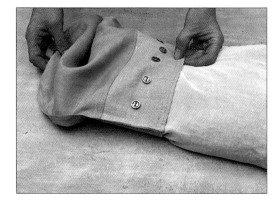

5 Make the inner sachet by folding the voile in half widthways and sewing around two sides to form a bag. Turn through, fill with lavender, fold in the edges of the last side and topstitch to close. Slip into the cover.

PANSY BOX

 Pansies press extremely well as the flowers are flat to start with. They come in a vast range of vibrant colours, which will soften a little when dried, often to more mellow tones. Keep them away from sunlight to avoid further fading. This papier-mâché box has been decorated with pansies, then varnished for protection. It's a pretty idea that can be adapted to decorate all manner of things, from stationery and greetings cards to pieces of furniture.

MATERIALS

wallpaper paste

bowl

newspaper

plain box

gold tissue paper

patterned tissue paper

pressed pansies

acrylic spray varnish

1 Mix the wallpaper paste according to the instructions on the packet. Tear the newspaper into small rectangles. Dip a piece of newspaper into the paste, ensuring it is thoroughly soaked, and apply it to the box, smoothing out any bubbles. Continue until the box is covered with a layer of papier mâché. Allow to dry out thoroughly over 24 hours.

2 Tear the gold tissue paper into small pieces and apply in the same way as the newspaper to cover the box. Allow to dry.

3 Tear the patterned tissue paper into squares that are just a little larger than the size of the pressed pansies. Use the paste to stick a square of tissue to the centre of each face of the box.

4 Carefully dip each pansy into the paste and apply in the same way as the paper squares, making sure the petals are flat and uncreased. Allow to dry thoroughly.

5 Spray the box and the lid with a coat of acrylic varnish to protect the decoration. Keep the finished box away from bright sunlight as the pansies could eventually fade.

DRIFTWOOD COATHOOKS

 It is not difficult to find pieces of driftwood that have a hooked shape, and they can easily be turned into a wonderful set of coathooks, all for the price of a few screws.

MATERIALS
tape measure
long piece of driftwood or reclaimed wood
drill
small hook-shaped pieces of driftwood
2 pieces of driftwood, about 15cm/6in
long screws
screwdriver

2 Drill corresponding holes in the bottom of each hook, and in the two mounting blocks. Drill some holes in the top of the mounting blocks for attaching to the wall. Screw the hooks firmly into position.

1 Measure the length of the long piece of driftwood and divide this by the number of hooked pieces to work out the spacing. Measure and mark the position of each hook. Drill using a bit compatible with the screws.

3 Screw the mounting blocks into position on the back of the main piece, near each end.

LAVENDER WREATH

 This glorious lavender wreath, bound with seagrass, makes an aromatic room decoration that will last all year. It needs to be made with lavender that is freshly picked and pliable.

MATERIALS
FOR A 45CM/18IN DIAMETER WREATH:

garden wire

wire cutters

medium-gauge florist's reel wire

about 250 stems of fresh lavender

green raffia

scissors

seagrass or similar thick string

2 Continue binding the bunches to the ring with wire. Pack them closely together to create a lush ring.

1 Make a 36cm/14in in diameter ring using three thicknesses of garden wire and bind with florist's reel wire. Make 30 bunches of six heads of lavender. Bind the first bunch of lavender on to the ring with wire.

3 Once bunches of lavender are wired on all around the ring, add more bunches but tie these into position using green raffia so that the wire is hidden. To finish, wind the seagrass string loosely around the wreath, and complete with a bow.

FRUITFUL EARLY AUTUMN

Season of mists and mellow fruitfulness,
Close bosom-friend of the maturing sun;
Conspiring with him how to load and bless
With fruit the vines that round the thatch-eaves run.

JOHN KEATS (1795-1821)

ABOVE: Autumnal fruits and flowers in perfect harmony.

LEFT: In early autumn, the orchard fruits are ready to harvest.

Autumn is the season of abundance. Leaves still adorn the trees and shrubs, but now they share the laden boughs with plump, ripe fruits, berries and seedcases. The hedgerows are bright with full red rosehips and glistening juicy blackberries, and entwined with the soft fluff of old-man's-beard (*Clematis vitalba*). As summer turns to autumn, the earth is still warm and some garden plants, such as Michaelmas daisies (*Aster*), chrysanthemums and Japanese anemones (*Anemone hupehensis*) have yet to bloom.

While there's a sense of pathos when we feel the first nip in the morning air that marks the end of summer, nature herself seems to rejoice

BELOW: Glistening rosehips are nature's own jewels, adorning the hedgerows.

as misty mornings and autumn rainfall give her a last chance to swell the fruit and produce the intense colours of autumn foliage and flowers. Early autumn offers a glorious palette of deep purples, burgundies, russet, oranges and greens. As flowers such as hydrangeas, left over from the summer, gently dry on their stems, their bright pastel pinks and blues mellow to softer shades of old rose and russet.

The other enduring image of early autumn is the harvest. Sheaves of golden corn and the sweet smell of fully ripened apples, pears and plums symbolize the fruition of the year's work. Since humans first began to cultivate the land, harvest has been the time when farming communities could take stock and assess whether there was plenty of food to take them through the winter, or whether the times ahead would be hard. In farming communities of times gone by, when a good harvest was believed to lie in the lap of the gods, many rituals and traditions grew up around the harvest.

It was thought that the corn spirit retreated as the field was harvested, and came to rest in the last sheaf where it would sleep through the winter. The corn spirit needed to be pleased, so this last sheaf would be cut and plaited (braided) into a corn dolly (decorative straw figure), then given a place of honour in the local

ABOVE: Ornamental cabbages are at their best in autumn, in gorgeous shades of blue-green and purple.

tavern. The following spring, the sheaf would be brought back to the field at seed time so the spirit could again bring about the germination of the new crop.

Once the crops had been gathered in, there was great jubilation as the Harvest Home was celebrated, with the farmer treating the workers to much eating, drinking and merriment. Farming and country communities still celebrate

ABOVE: Collect apples before strong autumn winds blow them off the trees.

RIGHT: Newly picked plums have an evocative dusty-looking bloom.

their year's achievement with village fairs, staging competitions for the largest or most perfect specimens of all manner of fruit and vegetables. Harvest Festival is also an important date in the church calendar when thanks are given to God in village churches for the bounteous gifts that fill granaries and larders.

This is the time for seasonal displays of sheaves and corn dollies (decorative straw figures), and fresh arrangements that combine the full richness of autumn: glorious fruit and vegetables amongst the season's leaves and flowers.

TRADITIONAL CORN DOLLY

 Despite their intricate appearance, corn dollies (decorative straw figures) are not difficult to make once you have mastered the art of working a five-straw plait (braid). Corn dollies can be made from many types of straw, but the best is long, hollow-stemmed wheatstraw. Look for ones with the longest section from the ear to the first "knot" where the leaf parts from the stem.

sheaf of long hollow-stemmed wheat
secateurs (pruners) or scissors
short length of raffia
2 dried oak leaves

1 To prepare the straws: remove the leaves, cut off each straw just above the first knot, then soak them in water for about 15 minutes. Remove the straws from the water, then stand them upright to drain. Tie five straws together near the ears using raffia. With the ears pointing downwards, spread out the straws like the spokes of a wheel. Working anti-clockwise (counter-clockwise), pass the first straw over the next two straws (the second and third), to occupy the space between the third and fourth straws. Go back one straw (to what is the third straw) and pass this straw over the next two straws.

LEFT: The traditional dolly, or "neck", is not difficult to make, using the basic five-straw plait, and once you've mastered it you will be able to create endless variations on the theme.

2 Then go back one straw and pass that straw over the next two straws. If you were to continue in this way, you would end up with a basic five-straw plait (braid), but to create the shape of this dolly, you need to begin to widen it out.

3 To widen out the shape, carefully bend the first straw over the second to lie outside the third straw. This is to ensure the fold in the first straw is facing away from the plait to begin to widen it.

4 *Then bring the first straw just inside the third, butting the first straw up to the edge of the bend in the third straw. Continue making rounds in this way, and you will find the dolly gradually widens out.*

5 *When you get to the end of a straw, snip it near a corner. Insert a new straw inside the hollow of the old one and continue to plait (braid). When you want to narrow the dolly, bring each successive corner fold to the inside of the last, just as it was brought outside the last to widen. Once it has narrowed down to a point, finish with a long straight plait, loop it around and tie. Trim with oak leaves.*

WHEATSHEAF TRADITIONS

 The simplest wheatsheaves are the most beautiful. Long straight straws tied in the middle with twine make a balanced and pleasing sheaf. This simple image has come to symbolize the harvest, which probably adds to its universal appeal. However, it is also traditional to add other autumn foliage, nuts and flowers for more elaborate sheaves whose beauty lies in their varied textures.

RIGHT: A sheaf of oats, oak leaves and maize, tied to a gatepost or fence, makes a pretty and lasting seasonal welcome for autumn visitors.

BELOW: To make the sheaf, first tie the oak branches on to the oats using raffia, then add the maize (corn). Add the decorative seagrass binding only once you're sure the sheaf is secure.

ABOVE: Barley, with its feathery ears and long straight stems, makes a striking sheaf. Twist the stems slightly to make them splay out at the top and bottom — both for greater impact and to give the whole ensemble a stable foundation. This sheaf has been tied with raffia, then given a belt of a five-strand plait (braid) made of seagrass as a final elegant detail.

LEFT: To make the seagrass plait, tie five strands together at one end, then lay them all parallel to each other over your hand. Take the right-hand strand and weave it over and under the other strands. Take the strand that is now furthest to the right and repeat, and so on, keeping the plait as taut as you can. Finish by tying the ends together in a knot.

HOP MANTEL GARLAND

 Hop bines (vines) are gloriously wild-looking, with delicate green flowers that seem to dance along their full length. Reaching up to 7m/23ft, bines make an ideal base for an autumn garland, whether it's around a door or across a mantel for a party, or over a church porch or churchyard gate for a wedding. Look out for them in early autumn when they are being harvested, as they are more pliable while they are still fresh. Hops are also available dried and can be revived and made more pliable with a spritz of water just before you are ready to arrange them.

MATERIALS

hooks or nails

hammer

pliers

florist's reel wire

hop bine (vine)

12 or more hard Conference pears

picture framer's gilt wax

heavy-gauge stub (floral) wires

RIGHT: Golden pears, with their curvaceous lines and smooth skins, make an excellent foil for the delicate-looking pale green hops.

1 Arrange hooks, nails or other suitable attachments either side of the fireplace. Use florist's reel wire to secure the complete bine (vine) to the mantel shelf.

2 Using your fingers, rub each pear all over with picture framer's gilt wax, allowing a little of the pear's natural skin tones to show through.

3 Pass a heavy-gauge stub (floral) wire through the base of each pear and twist the ends together. Use the wires to attach the pears to the bine base by winding them around the stems of the bine.

HARVEST DISPLAY

The soft blue-green shades of dried lavender stalks look impressive when massed together in a simple arrangement. Here, they have been teamed with golden wheat and dried poppy seed heads in a tin container whose gentle grey tones offset the blues, greens and golds perfectly. If you cannot find an old tin, use any galvanized metal for a similar effect.

MATERIALS
kitchen knife
4 dry florist's foam bricks
tin container, about 23 x 23 x 30 cm/
9 x 9 x 12 in
2 bunches dried barley
6 bunches dried lavender
2 bunches dried poppy seed heads
2 handfuls reindeer moss

1 Fit the florists' foam into the container, using the kitchen knife to trim to size. If you are using a tall container, stand two foam bricks upright in the bottom to support the two on top. The bricks on top must fit the container tightly.

Above: A sheaf of barley is an enduring symbol of the harvest safely gathered in. Long-stemmed varieties of grain crops like this are usually available only from craft suppliers.

2 Insert the barley, a few stalks at a time, into the centre of the foam. Discard any broken or imperfect stems.

3 *Working in rows, insert the lavender stalks one by one around the barley. Graduate the height of the rows of lavender so that the front ones are slightly lower than the back ones. This gives the impression of a more generous band of lavender.*

4 *Cut the stalks of the poppy seed heads to about 5 cm/2 in. Insert a row all around the rim of the container. Place another row behind them to rest on top. Tuck the reindeer moss carefully under the front row, lifting the seed heads a little if necessary.*

155

CABBAGE CANDLE RING

In autumn, there's a wide choice of ornamental cabbages, with leaves in wonderful colour combinations. Here, blue-green leaves shot with purple have been used to make a simple but striking candle-ring.

MATERIALS
kitchen knife
florist's foam block
pillar candle
plate
ornamental cabbage

1 Cut a square block from the florist's foam large enough to fix the candle in, leaving a margin of about 1cm/½in all round. Thoroughly soak the foam in water, allow to drain and place it in the middle of the plate, then push the candle into the centre.

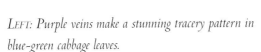

LEFT: *Purple veins make a stunning tracery pattern in blue-green cabbage leaves.*

2 Trim away the top edge of the block all around the candle. Break the leaves off the cabbage and, working from the bottom, push them face up into the sides of the florist's foam.

3 For the top layer, have the underside of the leaves uppermost to make them fan away from the candle.

156

AUTUMN SIDE DISPLAY

The soft greens and purples of early autumn make for breathtaking displays, and at this time of year there's a wonderful variety of flowers and fruits as well as foliage to work with. This arrangement combines all three, using tiny terracotta pots to add structure as well as to contain the smaller fruits.

MATERIALS
2 blocks florist's foam
kitchen knife
large bowl
4 small terracotta pots
secateurs (pruners)
bunch of oak leaves
blackberries and blueberries
3 ornamental cabbages
3 artichokes
3 flowering artichokes

RIGHT: Cabbages, blueberries and artichokes, usually more at home on the greengrocer's stall, make a voluptuous autumn display.

1 Soak the florist's foam and cut it to fit the bowl. Arrange the pots in the bowl, pushing them into the foam. Add stems of the oak leaves all around the edge of the bowl.

2 Fill the terracotta pots with the blackberries and blueberries. Position the ornamental cabbages in between the pots of fruit.

3 Complete the arrangement with the artichokes.

HYDRANGEA FRUIT BOWL

 The colours of hydrangea flowers gradually soften as summer turns to autumn, fading into increasingly subtle tones. The green varieties retain a verdant quality, even when they are fully dried, while the more colourful summer blooms take on fabulous old rose shades. These are colours that look glorious with autumn fruit such as plums and figs, so here they have been used to create an unusual presentation for an attractive autumn dessert.

MATERIALS
florist's foam ring, 40cm/16in in diameter
green serving plate
10 hydrangea heads and leaves
secateurs (pruners)

1 Soak the florist's foam ring in water. Place the plate in the middle of the ring. Cut the hydrangea stems to about 2.5cm/1in.

2 Arrange the hydrangea heads in the ring to cover the foam and add a few leaves for relief.

LEFT: Purple and green may seem an unlikely colour combination, but here it is arresting.

ROSEHIP WREATH

By early autumn, rosehips have ripened to their glorious best. Climbing and rambling roses produce long trailing branches of pretty rosehips that can easily be twisted into an enchanting wild-looking wreath. Be careful of any sharp thorns when you are working.

MATERIALS
florist's reel wire

trailing stems of rosehips

secateurs (pruners)

1 Using the wire, bind together the ends of two long stems of rosehips.

2 Bind the other two ends together to make a circle. You may wish to use three stems to make up the circle.

3 Add extra stems where the wreath needs extra fullness by twisting them into the frame.

LEFT: Varieties of roses that have attractive glossy rosehips like these should not be dead-headed in the summer if you want the hips to develop.

DECORATIVE FRUIT

Fruit is abundant in autumn, and symbolic of the season, so use it in witty and decorative ways – both for table and side displays and for imaginative food decorations. The seasonal glut makes this inexpensive and even if you make a mistake the fruit won't be wasted: you can just eat it, juice it or use it in cooking delicious fruit pies and tarts.

RIGHT: Carved lemons look pretty displayed in a bowl and can make a decorative garnish. Carve them using a cannelle knife (fine linoleum cutting tool). Make swirly patterns like these, or try geometric checks, which look just as effective.

BELOW: Serve pears a cut above the rest by carving stripes on them with a sharp paring knife. Brush lemon juice on to the cut areas to keep the flesh white.

RIGHT: Symbolic of love, apples make a witty display when given lips. Choose apples that do not have too high a sheen, but do have an attractive colour combination such as russet and green so the lips show up well. Apply a generous layer of russet-orange lipstick to your own lips and kiss the apples to make an imprint. Tuck each one in a basket and arrange them in a group.

FRUIT PRINT CALICO CUSHION

Very effective yet incredibly easy to do, fruit shapes in autumn shades look crisp and modern when printed on simple calico cotton. This cushion has a different design on each side, using the same apple and pear motifs for a co-ordinated look.

MATERIALS

2 x 50cm/20in squares of calico, plus a
spare piece

fabric paint in apple green, yellow and bronze

apple cut in half lengthways through stem
and core

pear cut in half lengthways through stem
and core

damp cloth

fabric pen in dark brown or black

sewing machine

matching thread

scissors

iron

30cm/12in square cushion pad

tailor's chalk

RIGHT: A more random design lends a fifties' feel.

1 Try out the printing on spare calico. Then smear the apple green or yellow fabric paint on to the cut surface of the fruit and print on to the cloth. Allow to dry.

2 Wipe the fruit clean using a damp cloth, apply the bronze paint and make a trial print on the cloth on top of the first print. Allow to dry.

3 Using the pen, sketch around the edge of each fruit print and also mark out the pip (seed) area. Use the pen lightly, allowing it to skip in places so the line is not too dark and hard.

4 Plan and print the design on the calico squares.
Allow to dry. With right sides together, sew around
three sides. Trim the corners, iron the seams open and
turn through to the right side. Slip the cushion pad in
and centre and mark the position of the edges of the
cushion with tailor's chalk, making sure the pad is
centrally placed.

   Take the cushion pad out and top-stitch through all
layers around the same three sides as before. Replace the
pad. Turn in and slip-stitch the raw edges of the open
end to close. Top-stitch all around just inside the
outside edge. Top-stitch the fourth inner seam and
top-stitch a second line of stitching all around just
outside the inner line.

RIGHT: *Simple lines of apples and pears make for a
crisp modern design.*

ROSEHIP TREE

Gather a variety of rosehips from around the garden, then turn them into a delightful little tree to decorate house, garden or patio. You'll need a stout pair of gardener's gloves, as many of the best hip-bearing shrub roses also have vicious thorns. Make this using wet florist's foam and it should last about a week.

MATERIALS
kitchen knife
florist's dry foam block
terracotta pot
bundle of willow osiers (branches)
secateurs (pruners)
florist's foam block or ball
gardener's gloves
selection of rosehips
moss

1 Cut the dry foam to fit securely in the pot. Trim the willow osiers (branches) to about 45cm/18in. Grasp them together at the bottom and push them into the centre of the foam in the pot.

2 Soak the other piece of florist's foam. If you are using a ball, simply push this on to the tops of the sticks. If you are using a block, first trim it to a ball shape before soaking.

LEFT: Rosehips from varieties such as 'Hansa', which are full and red, make a wonderful material for any autumn arrangement.

TIP
This beautiful rosehip tree will brighten any hallway or make a welcome decoration on your doorstep.

3 Wearing gloves, trim the branches of rosehips and push them into the foam. Cover the ball completely.

4 Dress the top of the pot with moss.

JARS OF AUTUMN COLOUR

 Autumn, like the sunset, puts on a glorious bright show, as if in an attempt to make up for the darker times that are to come. Yellows, golds, russet and the last of the greens vie for attention with the reds and oranges of berries and fruits. Autumn displays look best when they are not too mannered: just put them into jars and let them be.

BELOW: Branches of crab apples combine fabulously with russet beech leaves.

LEFT: *A jug of Chinese lanterns (*Physalis*), with their enchanting orange fruits set against green leaves, always makes an eye-catching autumn arrangement.*

ABOVE: *Autumn berries will happily mix. Here, a jar of waxy, translucent berries of the guelder rose (*Viburnum opulus*) is set off by a jar of mountain ash (*rowan*).*

LEFT: *Hydrangeas fade into subtle sepia tones during autumn. Here, several varieties have been combined with seasonal red berries for a pretty early autumn display.*

CRAB APPLE TABLE DECORATION

Crab apples have a special charm and the cultivated varieties produce fruit in a range of glorious colours. They make wonderful material for wild-looking arrangements such as this candle-ring. Make it up in wet florist's foam, and then let the whole thing dry out for a lasting autumn arrangement.

MATERIALS

florist's foam ring, 25cm/10in in diameter
4 yellow ochre tapered candles
secateurs (pruners)
2 branches crab apples
3 branches pin oak (*Quercus palustris*) leaves

1 Soak the florist's foam ring. Set the candles, evenly spaced, into the foam. Using sharp secateurs (pruners), cut the small branches of crab apples off the main stems. Arrange the oak leaves around the ring.

2 When the ring is covered with oak leaves, add smaller sprays to the inside.

3 Add the bunches of crab apples.

Left: *The yellows and russet of the crab apples and pin oak leaves are emphasized by the yellow ochre of the four tall, slim candles.*

LATE AUTUMN GOLD

Fair is the world, now autumn's wearing,
And the slippard sun lies long abed;
Sweet are the days, now winter's nearing
And all winds feign that the wind is dead.

WILLIAM MORRIS (1834-96)

ABOVE: A simple satin bow adds the finishing touch.

LEFT: The woods are at their most beautiful in the mellow midday autumn sun —
the perfect time to collect natural craft materials.

175

 Falling leaves are the enduring symbols of late autumn. They take on the most astounding colours, with vibrant oranges and golds marrying themselves to the greens of summer, and lighting up the horizon with their fiery colours.

Although the weather will really have broken by now, clear autumn days have a beauty all of their own. The low sun shines with a golden light, casting softer and longer shadows than in the brighter, harsher light of summer.

There is plenty to be harvested and preserved right now. The combination of the drying effect

LEFT: Golden autumn leaves are a universal icon of autumn.

BELOW: The gradual change into their autumn colours and dappled golden light combine to show the leaves at their most beautiful.

176

ABOVE: Oak leaves and acorns are to be found in plentiful supply in forests in the late autumn months.

of late summer and the slowing of growth in autumn means that much material is already semi-preserved. Capture the colours by pressing leaves for mounting in picture frames or between the pages of photograph albums, or even use them as natural decoupage. If you'd prefer more dimension for floral arrangements or temporary decorations for celebrations, let them air-dry into their own natural gently curled forms.

As shrubs and trees are stripped of their leaves, sticks and twigs become prominent again, just as they were in the spring – notably the rich burgundy red of the straight whip-like branches of dogwood (*Cornus*). Collect a few to make bird tables and houses, tea trays or decorative boxes.

Late autumn is also the season for pumpkins, squash and gourds, which come in a glorious array of colours from hot red to cool blue-greens. These can be simply piled up for autumn displays, or carved for seasonal celebrations.

As the nights draw in, late autumn is the ideal time to put preserved summer material to good use by making wreaths, topiaries and arrangements from dried flowers and grasses.

QUICK LEAFY DECORATIONS

The glorious shades and sheer abundance of leaves in autumn make them an irresistible material for use in decorations. The advantage they have over summer leaves is that, being dried out by the time they fall, they will retain their beauty for considerably longer. Use leaves for table or window decoration when entertaining, or for special autumn celebrations. Although autumn leaves are surprisingly resilient and will last some time if handled with care (or preferably not handled at all), they will eventually crumble, so enjoy them while they last.

ABOVE: Decorate an autumn table with a cloth made from finest golden tulle laid over a scattering of autumn leaves.

LEFT: Give glasses a party feel by tying large oak leaves around them with pieces of the finest green raffia or similar twine. This looks especially good on amber-coloured tumblers.

RIGHT: Create a natural curtain by tying bundles of autumn leaves together and hanging them at the window on fine twine. More leaves can be stuck lightly to the window frame to give the impression they are falling to the ground. Attach the leaves with sticky tack, using the smallest blob at either end of the main stem or vein.

WOODLAND TOPIARY

There's something immensely appealing about oak leaves and acorns, probably linked to fairy tales we heard as children. There are plenty of acorns to be gathered in the autumn, both in the countryside and in city parks. You'll need to collect small sprays of leaves, some complete with their acorns.

MATERIALS

florist's dry foam ball, 10cm/4in in diameter

10cm/4in terracotta pot

oak leaf sprays

pliers

acorns

heavy-gauge stub (floral) wires

1 Place the foam ball in the pot. Prepare the leaves by trimming the stems to 1cm/½in. Try to retain acorns on as many sprays as possible.

2 Make a ring of leaves around the top of the pot.

LEFT: These acorn cups make an interesting alternative to the common smoother ones.

3 Cut each stub (floral) wire into three equal lengths and push one into the base of each loose acorn and bend the end downward.

4 Push the wired acorns into the florist's foam. Continue adding leaves and acorns until the foam ball is completely covered.

WILLOW BIRD TABLE

This enchanting wigwam-style bird table made from willow twigs is ideal for smaller birds. It's easy to make, and the raffia used to bind it should hold through the winter, though you may like to re-bind the table for next winter before the raffia begins to disintegrate.

MATERIALS
secateurs (pruners)
large bundle of willow osiers (branches)
raffia

1 Cut 32 lengths of willow 23cm/9in long from the osiers (branches). Fold a length of raffia in half and place the end of the first stick in the fold. Twist the two ends of the raffia and place another stick next to the first. Continue weaving in this way until you have used 24 sticks. Tie the raffia ends. Weave more raffia around the other ends of the sticks to create the base.

2 Place another stick on top of the base, along the woven line. Take another piece of raffia, fold it in half and place the fold over the loose stick, passing the two ends between the base sticks and either side of the original weaving.

3 Turn the whole thing over and tie together as shown. Now pass one end between the next two sticks, over the loose stick and back to the underside of the base. Tie. Continue until the whole length of the reinforcing stick has been bound firmly to the base. Repeat at the other end. Next, make the short table walls. Place a stick across the ends of the bound-on sticks and tie at the corners using raffia. Repeat at the other end. Repeat with another pair of sticks placed at right-angles to the first, in line with the bound-on sticks. Finally, tie on another pair at right-angles again.

LEFT: *Made only with natural materials, this bird table is in keeping with its wild garden setting.*

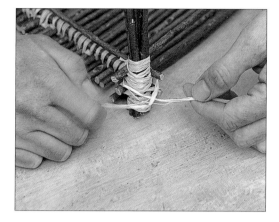

4 *Cut 32 lengths from the top of the osiers, each about 75cm/30in long. Divide these into four bundles of eight. Bind each bundle firmly at the bottom with raffia. Place the first bundle at one corner where the wall sticks project. Tie the bundle firmly to all the sticks. Repeat at the other three corners.*

5 *At the top, gather together the four bundles to create a wigwam shape and tie with raffia where they cross. Make a hanger by passing a few strands of raffia between the sticks, just under the raffia binding. Bring up and tie just above the binding, then tie the ends together for hanging.*

183

TRANSLUCENT LEAF LAMPSHADE

Skeletonized leaves have a translucent, ethereal quality, and make delightful decorative materials. You can either skeletonize the leaves yourself or buy them – autumn is the time they become available. Here, they have been gilded so they stand out against a green-painted shade.

MATERIALS
decorator's sponge
green craft paint
plain fabric lampshade
picture framer's gilt wax
about 8 skeletonized leaves (or enough to go around the lampshade)
craft glue

1 Wet the sponge and squeeze out until just damp. Dip it into the paint, then wipe on to the lampshade.

2 Using your fingers, rub picture framer's gilt wax on to the leaves. Try out the leaves in position on the lampshade until you are happy with the design.

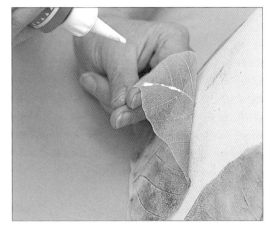

3 Apply glue sparingly to the back of a leaf and stick to the lampshade. Hold in position for a few seconds until the glue is dry.

4 Repeat with the other leaves until the lampshade is complete.

LEFT: Skeletonizing brings out the form of the leaves.

DRIED GRASS CIRCLET

There's something beguiling about this simple circlet of dried grass — symbolic, perhaps, of food and life itself. In the long dark evenings of late autumn, there is more time to transform material dried during the summer into decorative pieces for the home.

MATERIALS
1m/39in gardener's wire
florist's (stem-wrap) tape
about 30 large grass heads, or more
smaller ones
secateurs (pruners) or scissors
raffia

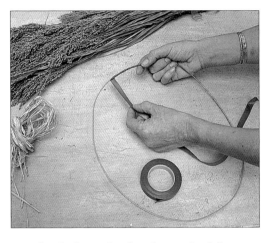

1 Make a hook at each end of the wire, bend the wire into a circle and hook the ends together. Bind the circle with florist's (stem-wrap) tape.

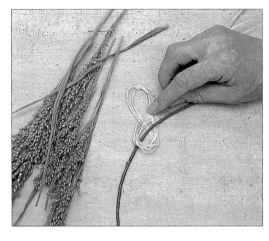

3 Fold a piece of raffia in half, pass both loose ends around the wire and back through the loop to fix (attach) it to the circlet.

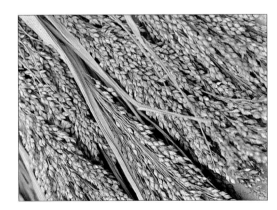

ABOVE: Choose the lushest grasses you can find, and don't cut off all the leaves as these lend texture to the finished piece.

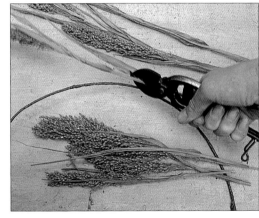

2 With a pair of sharp secateurs (pruners) cut the grass stems down to just below the first leaf from the top.

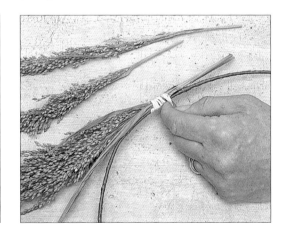

4 Take two grass heads and attach firmly with the raffia to the outside of the circlet, binding them at the top of the stems just under the seeds.

5 *About 7.5cm/3in along from the first binding, add two more heads to the inside of the circlet and bind. Repeat until the circlet is completely covered. Tie the ends of the raffia firmly to secure them.*

*N*OTE
Although grasses are very attractive, bear in mind that their green colour has a very short life, and most dry out to a warm, golden yellow colour. Always buy your grasses from a reputable dried flower supplier.

LEAF PRINT BOXES

Autumn leaves make delightful templates that can be used in a very simple way to decorate all manner of things. Choose interesting shapes, such as these deeply lobed oak leaves, and the end result is bound to be beautiful.

MATERIALS
plain cardboard box
matt emulsion (flat latex) paint in blue-grey
and cream
paintbrushes
pin oak leaf (*Quercus palustris*)
common oak leaf (*Quercus robur*)
stencil brush
newspaper
acrylic varnish

BELOW: This blue-grey and cream leaf colour combination makes an elegant alternative to more conventional autumn shades.

1 Paint the box inside and out with grey matt emulsion (flat latex) paint and allow to dry. Use the leaves to try out a design, and work out where you will place each motif.

2 Dip the tip of the stencil brush into the cream paint, then dab off the excess on a piece of scrap newspaper. Hold a large leaf on the side of the closed box and stipple the paint around its margins to make a clear imprint. Repeat all around the side of the box.

3 Repeat the large leaf motif in the middle of the top of the lid. Now use the small oak leaf in the same way to stencil a border around the top of the lid. Dab a little extra cream paint wherever there are large areas of grey between the leaves. Aim to apply a very thin veil of paint that allows the grey to show through, giving the impression of texture.

4 Once the paint is dry, apply a thin coat of varnish to all surfaces, inside and out, and allow to dry.

FALLING LEAF CURTAIN

A delightful sheer curtain with pockets for autumn leaves: the simple shapes of beech leaves have been used to complement the more elaborate oak leaves. It is very easy to make.

MATERIALS
scissors
white cotton organdie to fit window, plus
three-quarters as much again for
pockets and tabs
sewing machine
matching sewing thread
selection of autumn leaves
dressmaker's pins
curtain clips

LEFT: *Deeply lobed oak leaves make a pretty silhouette.*

1 Cut the organdie to fit the window, plus an allowance of 2.5cm/1in all around for the hem. Stitch a double hem all around. Lay the curtain on a flat surface and arrange the leaves on the curtain. Cut rectangles from the remaining organdie, a little larger than each leaf. Stitch a double hem around each piece.

NOTE
The autumn leaves in this project are naturally dried and therefore fully preserved. Although they are brittle, tucked into a sheer curtain that is not moved about, they are unlikely to get damaged.

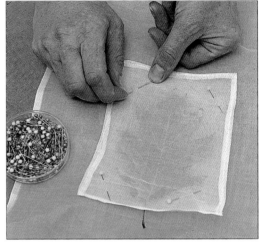

2 Pin each rectangle over its leaf and stitch the two sides and the base, leaving the top free. The leaves will probably fall out during this process.

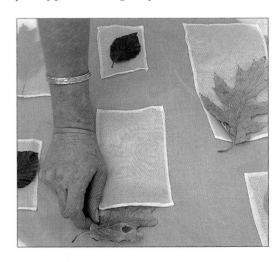

3 Replace each leaf in its pocket. Hang the curtain using curtain clips, or make tabs for the top edge.

ABOVE: The pockets are cut to fit each individual leaf and then the leaves are simply dropped into position.

SILVERY MIRROR FRAME

The glistening silvery medallions of honesty (*Lunaria*) (silver dollars) look wonderful woven into a dense frame for a mirror. The end result is light and delicate-looking while retaining an organic feel. Honesty grows prolifically in the hedgerows and, if allowed, in cottage-style gardens in temperate climates. The purple flowers of summer are replaced by uninspiring grey-looking medallion seedpods. However, when you remove the seedcases, you are left with a silvery membrane that makes a lovely decoration. It is far more resilient than it looks, but it is nevertheless best to use honesty where it won't have to stand up to daily wear and tear.

MATERIALS
garden wire

wire cutters

round mirror, ready-drilled, plus attachments

pliers

florist's (stem-wrap) tape

as much honesty (silver dollars) as you can collect

50cm/20in ivory organza

1 Cut enough wire to make a circle about 5cm/2in diameter smaller than the mirror. Make a hook at each end of the wire, join into a circle, then bind all of it.

2 Remove the seedcases from the honesty (silver dollars) and cut it into branched lengths of about 18cm/7in. Use the florist's (stem-wrap) tape to bind one length to the wire circle.

3 Place the next length of honesty a little lower than the first but so that the main stem lies over the main stem of the first piece. This way, you'll be able to create a dense mass of honesty. Continue to add lengths of honesty until the circle is completely covered. Next, you need to cover and bind the green-wrapped wire base.

4 Cut a strip of organza about 5cm/2in wide and thread it between the honesty medallions. Cut three lengths of garden wire 15cm/6in long. Bend the sharp cut ends in, then bind with a strip of organza.

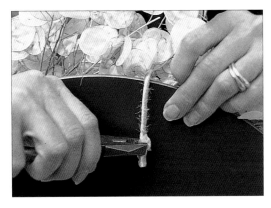

5 Make a small forward-bending hook at one end, and hook this to the wire base of the wreath. Bend the wire over the top of the mirror. Repeat with the other two pieces of wire, positioning them near the bottom. Hang the mirror, and make a generous bow from the remaining organza to trim the wreath.

LEAF DECOUPAGE BIN

It is satisfying to use leaves in place of paper images for decoupage boxes, bins or even furniture. The trick is to press the leaves first to ensure they are very flat and, once they are stuck on, to use layer upon layer of varnish until the leaf looks as if it is part of the surface.

MATERIALS
acrylic craft paint in green and yellow
MDF (medium-density fibreboard) waste bin
paintbrushes
crackle glaze
PVA (white) glue
large pressed leaf
weights or books
acrylic varnish

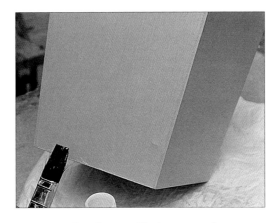

2 Different brands of crackle glaze are used in very different ways, so follow the manufacturer's instructions and try out the product first on the bottom of the bin. Paint one or two coats of crackle glaze on the outside of the bin. Allow to dry.

4 Apply PVA (white) glue to the back of the leaf, making sure you spread it to the very edges. Place the leaf in position, then rest heavy weights, such as books, on the leaf overnight. Remove the weights and allow the glue to dry fully.

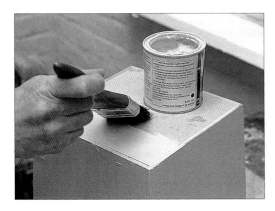

1 Paint the bin inside and out with soft green paint and allow to dry.

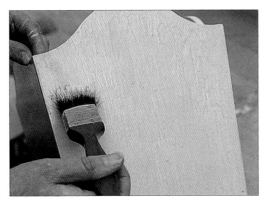

3 Very carefully lay on the second colour on the outside of the bin. The paint surface should crack as it dries. The size and type of cracks depend on the consistency of the top coat of paint.

5 Coat all the surfaces with a thin coat of acrylic varnish. Allow to dry thoroughly. Repeat with as many coats of varnish as needed, until the leaf appears to be painted on to the bin.

FILIGREE CARVED PUMPKIN

 This delicate tracery pattern is easier to carve than it looks and makes a pretty alternative to traditional jack-o-lanterns. Make several and bring them to life by placing night-lights (tea-lights) inside to create a row of decorations.

MATERIALS
pen

pumpkin

pumpkin saw or craft knife saw

attachment

kitchen knife

scoop or spoon

lino (linoleum) cutting tools

night-light (tea-light)

ABOVE: The wavy-edged lid is also given some simple decorative detailing.

1 Draw a wavy line around the top of the pumpkin to mark the edge of the lid then cut around this using the pumpkin saw. Use a sharp kitchen knife to cut out the centre of the lid for ventilation so that the lantern will burn while the lid is on.

2 Scoop out all the seeds and flesh using a kitchen spoon. Scrape away the inside to make a thin "shell".

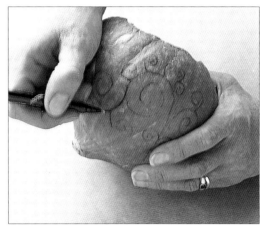

3 Draw an all-over tracery pattern on the skin of the pumpkin, working circles and curlicues freehand.

4 Use lino (linoleum) cutting tools in a range of thicknesses to cut out the pattern. Try out the night-light (tea-light) to check the light shines through. If not, scrape away a little more of the inside of the shell.

SIMPLE PUMPKIN CARVING DESIGNS

The scope for pumpkin and squash carving is endless, and it need not be difficult. Abstract designs are often the easiest choice for beginners as you really can't go wrong – all you need to do is simply add a few extra flourishes to fill in any gaps. Geometric designs are slightly more complicated as you need to plan them carefully to get full repeats around the whole circumference of the pumpkin.

The best solution is to divide the pumpkin into quarters or eighths from top to bottom, marking the divisions with a pen, and work out a design that can be repeated in each section.

Geometric designs can also be worked out along evenly marked-out concentric circles drawn out around the pumpkin.

Figurative designs look good on pumpkins, too. They don't have to be complicated – simple lines work well. If you're unsure about drawing freehand, photocopy a simple image, then reduce or enlarge it to fit the pumpkin. To transfer the image, pin the drawing or photocopy to the pumpkin, then mark out the design using a large needle or pricking tool to prick through the paper on to the skin of the pumpkin, following the lines of the image. Remove the paper, leaving a line of holes to carve along.

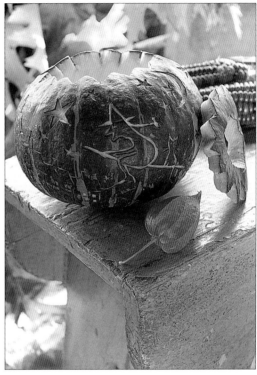

ABOVE: Witches are an alternative to jack-o-lanterns, while keeping to the traditional Halloween theme.

LEFT: Keep carving simple on smaller pumpkins, lending variety with slits, zig-zags and scrolls. Make several, then group them in a window display.

RIGHT: The peaceful features of this face make a simple but appealing image that is easy to transfer to a pumpkin. Lay her on a bed of leaves to give the impression of a woodland pillow.

ORGANIC CANDLE HOLDERS

Autumn fruits and vegetables offer wonderful possibilities for organic candle holders. Many have firm flesh that provides good support for candles and night-lights (tea-lights). They must have a good stable base, to avoid the risk of falling over while the candle is burning and causing a fire. If the pieces you choose don't easily sit straight, use a kitchen knife to shave a little off the bottom so that it is flat. Even so, never leave any candles burning unattended, especially next to flammable surfaces.

BELOW: Apples make charming little candle holders, and this is a good way to use up windfalls (extras). First slice a little off the bottom of each one to create a stable base, then hollow the fruit out using an apple corer. Enlarge the hole a little so that it is big enough to accommodate a night-light (tea-light).

ABOVE: The "fingers" of the Crown of Thomas gourd seem to be cradling this pillar candle. Some gourds have very hard flesh, so you'll need a sharp knife to hollow them out. Wrap the candle in an autumn leaf, tie with raffia and place in the holder. (It is safe to burn only large diameter candles wrapped in leaves as the wax burns from the middle, leaving the outer surface cool.)

RIGHT: Small green striped squashes look charming holding apple-green candle stubs and set on rustic earthenware plates. They're quick and easy to prepare — simply hollow out the centre with an apple corer, then insert the candle.

PRESSED LEAF PICTURE FRAMES

The sepia tones of autumn leaves can be used to make very simple organic photograph frames. To produce sepia photographs of your family, use black-and-white film (XR2) and ask the processors to put it through the ordinary colour process (C41).

MATERIALS
photograph
oval mount
clip frame
selection of pressed leaves
secateurs (pruners) or scissors
craft glue

1 Position the photograph and mount in the frame. Collect together pressed leaves to cover the frame.

2 Snip the stems off the leaves and try out the arrangement around the frame.

LEFT: *Press leaves for at least a week before using.*

3 Run a line of craft glue down the spine of each leaf and glue in position on the glass over the mount.

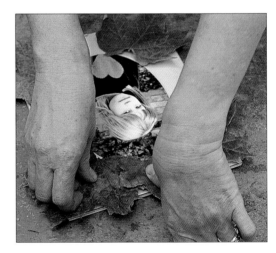

4 The leaves may need to be held firmly until the glue is almost set. Continue gluing until the mount is completely covered with leaves.

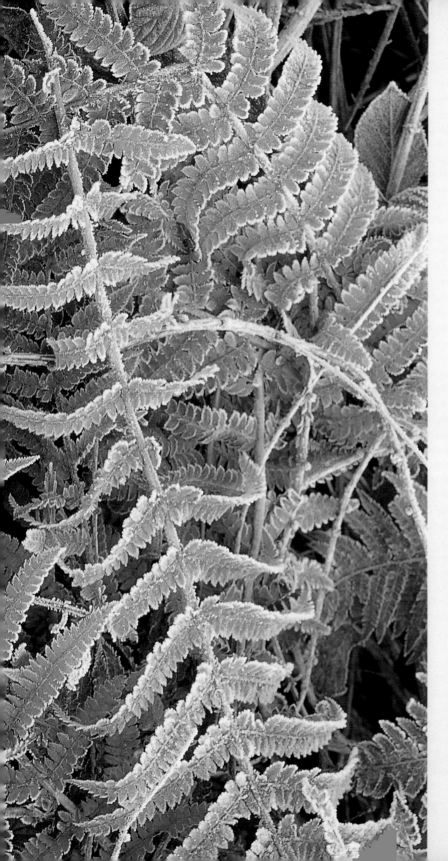

WINTER'S FROSTY DAWN

Every leaf speaks bliss to me
Fluttering from the autumn tree
I shall smile when wreaths of snow
Blossom where the rose should grow

EMILY BRONTË (1818-48)

ABOVE: A beautiful example of variegated holly leaves in all their glory.

LEFT: Hoar frost throws its translucent cloak of white over any remaining plant life, highlighting stems and veins.

Spreading his magnificent cloak of white over all that grows, Jack Frost announces winter is here. That beautiful first frosty morning sounds a silent death knell for autumn, putting deciduous plants to sleep for the winter. From now on, flowers will be few; fruits will be unable to survive and only the hardiest of berries will remain to provide colour for the garden.

This is the season when evergreens reign. Deep green and densely covered with needles, stately coniferous trees produce cones that range in size from little bigger than a plum stone (pit) to those that are fist-sized or even larger. Both branches and cones (pinecones) make brilliant craft materials, as do the glossy leaves of holly

BELOW: Frosted leaves reveal their delicate structure.

ABOVE: Stems of holly, stripped of their leaves, provide a fiery mass of colour in winter, especially if abundant branches are massed in a large jug.

and ivy. With this naturally lush and colourful fresh material, there is less need for dried or preserved material for decoration, but it does come into its own for making gifts.

Dried lavender, roses and spices can all be made into special scented treats for loved ones; the more brightly coloured dried flowers, such as yarrow, can be turned into a decoration that will recall an earlier, sunnier season.

The natural colours for decoration at this time of year are green and red. These can be lightened with variegated varieties of holly and ivy, which always add sparkle to arrangements. Variations on the red theme include fruits such as apples, cranberries and cut pomegranates which can be added to the berries of holly and pyracantha that are readily available outside throughout the winter months.

Right: The frosted undergrowth appears like sketchlines against the darker tones of the tree trunks.

Below: Frost dusts the contours of wild mushrooms, accentuating their shapes.

YARROW TREE

Yarrow (*Achillea millefolium*) dries beautifully, retaining its mellow old-gold tones. Each flower head provides a generous cushion of colour, making it very quick and easy to work with. Here, the dried seedheads of *Nigella orientalis* have been used to punctuate the yarrow for a rich textured look.

MATERIALS
kitchen knife
florist's dry foam block
yellow container
secateurs (pruners)
bundle of willow osiers (branches) or similar
about 45cm/18in long
florist's dry foam ball 18cm/7in in diameter
raffia
3 large bunches dried yarrow
1 bunch *Nigella orientalis*
dried autumn leaves

VARIATION
Other dried flowers which are suitable to arrange in this way are: *Paeonia*, *Protea compacta*, *Rosa*, *Achillea ptarmica*, *Anaphalis margaritacea* and *Helichrysum*.

1 Trim the foam block to fit into the container. Use secateurs (pruners) to trim the sticks to an even length.

3 Bind the osiers with two strands of raffia and tie securely at the base.

2 Hold the osiers (branches) in a bundle and drive them through the centre of the foam in the container. Push the florist's foam ball on to the osiers.

4 Cut the yarrow stems to about 2.5cm/1in and push them into the foam so that it is completely covered and no foam is visible.

5 *Cut the* Nigella orientalis *stems to about 5cm/2in and add to the ball at intervals.*

6 *Arrange a selection of dried autumn leaves in the foam in the container to completely cover it providing texture and interest.*

NATURAL GIFTWRAP

 Nature has plenty to offer that can be used to make imaginative giftwrap, especially early in winter when plant and seed material is inclined to be more robust than delicate fresh flowers. Think in terms of leaves, grasses, sticks and twigs to create thoughtful but inexpensive decorations for wrappings. All these materials look best against the simplest of papers, such as ordinary brown parcel wrap or the soft tones and robust texture of recycled papers. You'll also need some basic cotton string, seagrass or other simple twine that tones well with natural materials to use as ties.

ABOVE: Dogwood twigs, with their fabulous burgundy colouring and uncomplicated straight lines, make a modern decoration for a brown paper package. The bundle has been tied together using a natural leather thong, then bound on to the parcel with the same thong for an understated, clean look.

LEFT: Each naturally giftwrapped parcel is unique yet they also look good together, as demonstrated by this highly individual trio.

ABOVE: A parcel simply wrapped in robust recycled paper and tied with seagrass string is given an individual finish with the addition of two stems of dried grass.

RIGHT: Larch twigs covered with lichen have a beauty all of their own, with the diminutive cones set against the glorious silvery grey of the lichen. If you don't own such a tree, a florist should be able to supply suitable twigs at this time of year. This parcel has been wrapped in recycled paper with a layer of translucent glycerine paper on top to provide an interesting layered background for the larch. The whole ensemble has been tied together with ordinary cotton string.

211

NATURAL CARDS

 Handmade greetings cards convey more heartfelt sentiments than the bought variety, and nature offers some of the most beautiful forms for inspiration. Early winter is an excellent time to find plant material for these, as much of it is already dried. Collect leaves, seedheads and seedcases, dried flowers and twigs, and set out simple designs on recycled rag or bark papers.

LEFT: Use natural materials to create handmade greetings cards and gift tags.

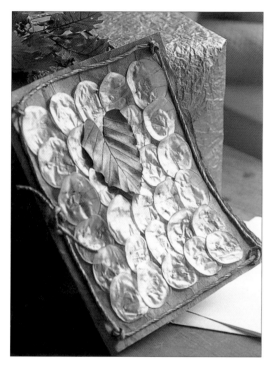

ABOVE: Simple yet delightful, this card is emblazoned with a beech leaf cut into a heart shape and mounted on a background of honesty (silver dollars).

LEFT: Tiny dried chrysanthemums are set in a simple geometric arrangement on a square of natural fibre paper, positioned high on the rag paper "card" to relieve the squareness of the design. All the paper has been torn by hand, rather than cut, to give softer edges.

RIGHT: A sprig of oak, tied with gold paper twine and attached to bark paper, makes a charming gift tag.

213

BLUE SPRUCE AND AMARYLLIS GARLAND

Deep pinks and raspberry shades are readily available in winter, and yet are often overlooked in a traditional preference for red. Here, the combination of frosty-looking blue spruce and lichen-covered twigs with translucent apple-green candles and the raspberry shades of the amaryllis and grapes, makes a refreshing winter colour scheme for a lavish garland.

MATERIALS

3 florist's foam blocks

kitchen knife

25cm/10in wide strip of chicken wire to fit mantel shelf

5 small metal buckets

secateurs (pruners)

2 branches blue spruce

glass nuggets or small pebbles

3 large green pillar candles

4 thin green pillar candles

fine raffia or twine

6 stems amaryllis (*Hippeastrum*)

10 sprays lichen-covered larch twigs

2 large bunches red grapes

RIGHT: Metal buckets hold candles and flowers, while adding to the silvery, frosty look.

1 Soak the florist's foam, cut each block in half lengthways and leave to drain. Arrange the cut blocks along the chicken wire. Wrap the chicken wire around the blocks leaving gaps for the buckets. Cut the spruce into manageable lengths and arrange in the florist's foam to create a base for the garland.

2 Place a large handful of glass nuggets or small pebbles in the bottom of each bucket, then secure one large candle in each of three of the buckets. Tie the thin candles into pairs using raffia or twine and set a pair in each of the remaining buckets. Add water, then two stems of amaryllis with each large candle.

3 Arrange the larch twigs amongst the spruce. Finally, split up the bunches of grapes and group some in front of each bucket.

ROSE AND SPICE POT-POURRI

 The rich aromatic combination of sweet-smelling rose, lavender and spices, makes a warm and inviting winter pot-pourri. By fixing the aroma with orrisroot, you should be able to enjoy the perfume of the pot-pourri all winter long. If you want to give the scent an instant boost (as people are arriving for a party, for example), sprinkle on a few drops of hot water from the kettle.

MATERIALS

picture framer's gilt wax

7 cinnamon sticks cut into thirds

18 star anise

6ml/120 drops lavender essential oil

3ml/60 drops geranium essential oil

2ml/40 drops clove bud essential oil

small bottle

2.5ml/½tsp ground nutmeg

25g/1oz ground orrisroot

mixing containers

25g/1oz whole cloves

15g/½oz dried mace

115g/4oz dried lavender

225g/8oz dried rosebuds

1 Rub picture framer's gilt wax on to the cinnamon sticks and star anise, and reserve.

BELOW: *Choose pretty two-toned peach and yellow roses to add brightness to the finished pot-pourri.*

2 Blend the essential oils in a bottle and shake. Add a little oil to the ground nutmeg and orrisroot and blend. Add the rest of the blended oils to the whole dried spices. Cover and leave in a dark place for 24 hours.

3 In a large bowl, mix the cinnamon sticks and star anise with the remaining ingredients and add the essential oil mixture. Cover and leave for six weeks in a dark place before using or packing as a gift.

POMANDERS

Traditional pomanders can be given a new, less manicured look by substituting raffia for ribbon and trimming them with a variegated holly leaf. For centuries, pomanders have been cured with orrisroot and dried out over several weeks in a warm dry place, such as an airing cupboard. The quicker alternative method is to dry them in the oven; although the pomanders are preserved this way, they come out a little softer than by the traditional method.

MATERIALS

soft-skinned oranges, such as navel

sharp vegetable knife

cloves

skewer

raffia

variegated holly leaves

1 Preheat the oven to 110°C/225°F/Gas ¼. Make slits in the skins of the oranges using a small sharp vegetable knife. This helps speed the drying process in the oven. Put a line of cloves either side of the slit. Continue to build up the design by making a row of cloves around the middle of the pomander, with another row either side of that.

TIP

If you are planning a geometric design, make slits at each quarter. If you wish to work a motif you may prefer to leave the front of the orange intact, and just make a slit in each side and one at the back. Geometric designs look good when the slits become part of the pattern.

LEFT: Ring the changes from the normal geometric shapes and make heart and star shapes instead.

2 Fill in the top and bottom of the orange with concentric circles of cloves.

3 Pass a skewer through the slits of the oranges and balance the skewer ends on the sides of a deep dish so that plenty of air can circulate around the oranges. Place the dish in the oven and leave for 12 hours, or until the oranges are completely dry. Tie a length of raffia around the pomander, making a hanging loop, and tuck a sprig of holly into the top.

APPLE AND IVY TABLE DISPLAY

 Shiny ruby-toned apples teamed with glossy berried ivy offer a bold alternative way to create the traditional winter colour scheme of green and red. Crab apples have been used to add extra detail to the arrangement.

MATERIALS

urn

plastic sheet

florist's foam block

kitchen knife

heavy-gauge stub (floral) wires

about 16 red apples

2 branches of crab apples

secateurs (pruners)

berried ivy sprigs

BELOW: Soft raspberry-coloured candles perfectly complement the colours of the apples.

1 Line the urn with a plastic sheet, soak the florist's foam, drain, then cut to fit tightly into the urn. Pass a stub (floral) wire through each apple and twist the ends together.

2 Make a circle of apples around the rim of the urn, securing them in the florist's foam with the wires. Make a second ring of apples on top of the first, then add one on top to create a dome.

3 Wire up the clusters of crab apples and add to the arrangement, positioning them in between the larger red apples. Trim the berried ivy stems and insert the stems into the foam.

4 Fill in any remaining gaps in the display with more wired crab apples.

HOLLY AND POMEGRANATE SIDE DISPLAY

Pomegranates are wonderfully visual winter fruits, especially when cut open to show off their glistening clusters of ruby seeds. Here, a classic winter display is given a new twist by choosing variegated holly and nature's own baubles in the form of pomegranates.

MATERIALS
florist's foam blocks
large shallow bowl
large bunch of variegated holly
secateurs (pruners)
bunch of holly berries (*Ilex verticillata*)
knife
6 pomegranates
24 heavy-gauge stub (floral) wires

ABOVE: Quartered pomegranates add a jewel-like quality to seasonal holly.

1 Soak the florist's foam, drain it and place in the bowl. Position a long piece of holly at the back of the arrangement and one at each side to create a fan shape.

2 Fill in with plenty of holly, trimming the stems to create a domed shape. Add stems of holly berries throughout the arrangement.

3 Quarter the pomegranates lengthways and pierce each one with a stub (floral) wire through the bottom end. Bend the end of the wire to secure.

4 Position the pomegranates carefully, inserting the wires into the florist's foam and bending them into position if necessary.

CRANBERRY HEART

 This glossy red heart made from cranberries and raffia has a wonderful contemporary feel. Cranberries are easy to find from late autumn right into the middle of winter. They retain their shiny brightness well for several weeks, though as the berries dry they will shrink a little.

MATERIALS

wire cutters

1m/39in garden wire

1 large punnet of cranberries

florist's reel wire

raffia

2 Bend the two circles into heart shapes. Put one heart shape inside the other and bind them together top and bottom using florist's reel wire.

3 Bind the hearts together using raffia, passing the raffia between the cranberries. Use the raffia to make a hanging loop at the top.

1 Cut the garden wire in half and make a small hook at one end. Thread cranberries on to the other end. When the wire is filled, make another hook and join together. Repeat with the other piece of wire.

WINTER'S SWEET REPOSE

And Winter slumbering in the open air,
Wears on his smiling face a dream of Spring!

SAMUEL TAYLOR COLERIDGE (1772-1834)

ABOVE: Winter jasmine produces surprisingly delicate-looking, but nevertheless hardy, yellow flowers on leafless stems all through the winter and into spring.

LEFT: A metal garden basket full of variegated holly brings seasonal cheer to the coldest of days.

227

As winter presses on and the land-scape retreats under a blanket of snow, dark evenings are the time to use dried material from the more abundant months. Dried beans, preserved leaves and flowers can all be made into gifts and decorations. The evergreens are still around, of course, and the traditional hollies and ivies can be supplemented with softer-toned eucalyptus for a lighter effect.

As the weeks progress, just as we're lulled into the impression that nature really has entered an everlasting sleep, she surprises us with flowers: winter-flowering jasmine (*Jasminum nudiflorum*) sprouts tiny golden blooms on green shoots whenever there's a mild spell in winter, right through to spring. Long-lasting hellebores, with their delicate nodding heads and subtle shades that span white to green, palest pink to softest burgundy, make their appearance late in winter

ABOVE: The waxy, white flowers of Helleborus niger *are winter's natural stars.*

and continue to flower right through to spring. But white and cream are the enduring colours of late winter, epitomized by the fragile-looking but brave snowdrop which pushes up through the snow. And as if somehow to sweeten the harshness of the season, many flowers, such as winter-flowering honeysuckle (*Lonicera purpusii*) and winter-flowering daphne (*Daphne odora*), not only look exquisite, they are also highly perfumed.

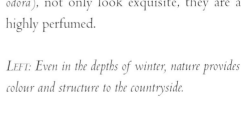

LEFT: Even in the depths of winter, nature provides colour and structure to the countryside.

ABOVE: Snow carpets the countryside, providing warmth and protection from harsh frosts.

In the deepest of winter, follow nature's lead and decorate your home using the purest of white flowers that will scent as well as decorate the room. Enhance their purity by displaying them in white containers that will also reflect the pale wintry light.

Plant up some of the early flowering bulbs to enjoy inside — as their vigorous shoots push through the earth, they are a symbolic reminder of the work nature is putting in behind the scenes. Soon this energy will be echoed outside as the first spring shoots appear. In the meantime, relish the burgeoning of life indoors and, when the bulbs do open, enjoy their heady natural scent.

EUCALYPTUS AND WHITE HELLEBORE RING

The blue-green leaves of eucalyptus have a frosty appeal, especially when teamed with seasonal white flowers such as these exquisitely beautiful hellebores (*Helleborus niger*). If you're unable to find these, you could substitute white anemones for a similar effect.

MATERIALS
kitchen knife
florist's foam ball, 18cm/7in minimum diameter
23cm/9in plate
4 church candles, 2.5cm/1in in diameter
scissors
bunch of small-leaved eucalyptus
16 *Helleborus niger* or white anemones

1 Cut the foam ball in half — or slice off a section if it is larger — to fit the plate. Soak it in water and allow to drain. Using the kitchen knife, cut the bottom ends off three of the candles to create varying lengths and snip the wicks with scissors. Push the candles into the centre of the foam.

LEFT: The purity of the candle-ring perfectly complements classic church candles.

2 Cut the eucalyptus into pieces about 15cm/6in long and arrange in the foam to cover it.

3 Cut the hellebore flower stems to about 12.5cm/5in long and add to the arrangement at random intervals.

EUCALYPTUS STAR

The pretty evergreen leaves of eucalyptus dry well, retaining their colour, though reducing slightly in size. This delicate star makes an attractive winter decoration that will gradually dry out and last for weeks.

MATERIALS
12 willow osiers (branches) about
60cm/24in long
secateurs (pruners)
florist's reel wire
small-leafed eucalyptus

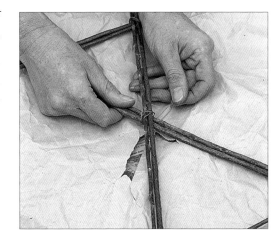

2 Place one triangle over the other to make a star shape and wire them together at all the points where the triangles cross.

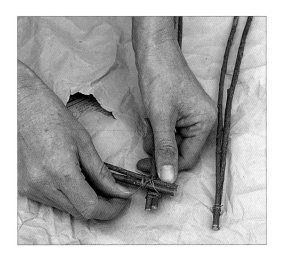

1 Trim the osiers (branches) to the same length and wire in pairs at each end. Wire three pairs of osiers together, making a triangle. Repeat with the other pairs.

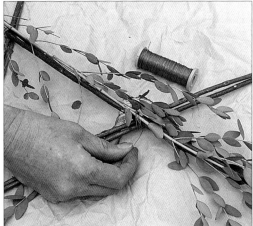

3 Wire lengths of eucalyptus to the willow to cover the star, but create a feathery finished effect.

WINTER CHANDELIER

Variegated holly always looks pretty and makes a robust yet delightful decoration for this wild winter chandelier. Here, thornless holly from the tops of the trees has been used as it is much easier to work with.

MATERIALS

large cones to fill the basket
newspaper
antique gold spray paint
ornate wire basket
variegated holly branches
secateurs (pruners)
florist's reel wire

2 Choose young branches of holly with small offshoots and fix them to the basket rim using florist's reel wire. The offshoots give depth to the rim.

1 First gild the cones. This should be done in a well-ventilated area. Shake the can well, then spray the cones and allow to dry. Place in the basket.

3 Using florist's reel wire, attach a generous sprig to the bottom of the basket.

234

EUCALYPTUS PYRAMID

This pretty pyramid of eucalyptus, set on a footed glass dish, makes a simple but impressive table display that's quick and easy to make. This pyramid has a dry foam base: the eucalyptus will go on looking fresh for a day or two, then gradually dry out for an everlasting arrangement.

MATERIALS
florist's foam cone, 20cm/8in high
footed glass dish
secateurs (pruners)
small-leaved eucalyptus sprigs
eucalyptus buds

2 Work up the cone, positioning the eucalyptus sprigs at a more upright angle as you work nearer to the top.

1 Place the foam cone on the footed dish, then cut some sprays of eucalyptus and arrange around the base.

3 When the cone is completely covered with foliage, add the frosty looking eucalyptus buds.

DRIED BEAN MOSAIC

Dried beans come in a glorious variety of shapes, sizes and colours, and make ideal material for a natural mosaic. The key to success is to work in concentric circles or straight lines.

MATERIALS

scissors

paper

14cm/5in square picture frame

pen

craft glue

mung beans

haricot beans (navy beans)

1 Cut a square of paper the same size as the frame back. Fold it in half and draw and cut out half a heart shape. At its widest points, the heart should be about 1.5cm/⅝in smaller than the frame. Position the heart centrally on the backing paper and draw around it.

3 Very carefully stick a line of mung beans along the line of glue. Squeeze another line of glue inside this and make another line of mung beans. Continue in this way, working in concentric rounds, until the whole heart is covered.

2 Squeeze a line of craft glue along the drawn line.

LEFT: *Two different sizes of bean contrast strikingly in this simple mosaic.*

4 Squeeze a line of glue around the outside of the heart and make a line of haricot beans (navy beans). Make another line outside this, then fill in the corners, laying on one bean at a time. Mount in the picture frame.

DRIED ROSE LOVE TOKEN

 Heart shapes are always appealing and this one, made from preserved green beech leaves and dried gold-coloured rosebuds, makes a delightful gift and a lasting decoration for any-where in the house.

MATERIALS
75cm/30in garden wire

pliers

florist's (stem-wrap) tape

florist's reel wire

sprigs of preserved beech leaves

12 dried yellow rosebuds

2 Bend the circle into a heart shape.

4 Cut 12 lengths of reel wire 5cm/2in long, and pass each one through the base of a dried rosebud. Twist the ends together.

1 Bend the length of garden wire into a circle, hooking the ends together. Bind the wire circle with the florist's (stem-wrap) tape.

3 Use florist's reel wire to attach the beech sprigs to the heart shape, bending the twigs to follow the shape as you wire them.

5 Wire the yellow rosebuds to the base, tucking in the wire ends at the back of the heart to create a neat finished piece.

EVERLASTING LEAF AND FLOWER ORBS

Leafy balls make delightful organic decorations. These have been made from preserved beech and oak leaves and preserved hydrangea flowers. Beech leaves are used as the base for the flower ball. For the leaf balls, simply rub the leaves first with a little picture framer's gilt wax, then follow the first two steps.

MATERIALS

picture framer's gilt wax
preserved beech leaves
glue gun and glue sticks
florist's dry foam ball 10cm/4in in diameter
preserved hydrangea heads
scissors

1 Apply a line of glue down the centre of a beech leaf and stick it to the foam ball. Repeat, to make a line of leaves around the circumference of the ball.

2 Filling in one side at a time, cover the ball completely with beech leaves.

LEFT: *Enhance the autumnal shades with toning ribbon.*

3 Rub the hydrangea florets with a little picture framer's gilt wax. Carefully snip the florets off their stems, leaving about 3mm (⅛in) stem.

4 Place a small blob of glue in the centre back of each flower and attach on top of the leaves, allowing the petals to curl naturally at the edges to give texture to the finished piece.

WINTER WINDOW DECORATIONS

 In winter, when light is precious, make a feature of your windows. Either bring in a little nature (in the form of branches or evergreen leaves) from outside and team it with candlelit lanterns to extend the light into the dusk, or seek out the whitest flowers you can find to bring lightness to the windowsills. Remember too that many white flowers in winter have beautiful scent. As winter progresses, there will be several varieties to choose from, such as snowdrops, paper-white narcissi and *Helleborus niger*.

BELOW: Bring brightness to a lichen-covered larch twig by rubbing picture framer's silver wax on to the cones. Hang the twigs at the window using string. Complete the display with a row of lanterns. For safety's sake, never leave lighted lanterns unattended, and don't draw curtains in front of them.

ABOVE: Trim window handles with a bouquet of paper-white narcissi: small bunches are tucked into orchid phials (vials) that have been wrapped in translucent organza ribbon.

RIGHT: Make a display of white flowers and vases for brightness on the windowsill.

WINTER POSIES

Although in the dead of winter few plants are in bloom, there are some that produce modest flowers, and these are all the more beautiful for their rarity. White is the favourite colour for late winter – notably, classic snowdrops and hellebores (*Helleborus niger*). Posies of the palest blooms, or grey-green foliage that looks as if it has been touched by frost, evoke the silent peacefulness of a crisp, clear winter's day when the landscape has been blanketed with snow. Their almost colourless petals seem to complement the gentle watery light of midwinter and inspire hope of the spring to come.

BELOW: Eucalyptus produces frosty-looking buds. Wrap them up with sprays of foliage in translucent glycerine paper to make a pretty winter bouquet.

ABOVE: White anemones fade to a fabulous antique ecru shade. Tie them with a toning ribbon and arrange them in a cream-coloured cup and saucer.

RIGHT: Exquisitely beautiful white hellebores (Helleborus niger) are all the more treasured as they are one of the few flowers to bloom in the dead of winter. However, they stay around long enough (well into spring) to be really appreciated and last well as cut flowers too. Make a feature of them by incorporating them in a display of glass and candles.

WINTER BULB DISPLAYS

Perhaps because there is so little evidence of life amongst plants in winter, the first shoots are all the more precious. As winter draws on, bulbs planted for indoor displays begin to shoot. For bulbs to flower earlier than in the ground you must plant them in the autumn and keep in a warm, dark place for about six weeks to encourage them to sprout. If you forgot to plant them up in autumn, look around florists and markets for pots planted with paper-white narcissi or hyacinths, then re-plant them in your own displays. They look wonderful even while they are still green, the vigorous shoots holding the promise of exquisite perfumed blooms. Once they are planted, it is astounding quite how fast they grow and the tall slender leaves look wonderful, even before the blooms appear.

ABOVE: Secure the leaves in position using florist's wire bent into a hairpin shape.

LEFT: A covering of autumn leaves over the top of narcissi bulbs will both protect the bulbs against the cold and make a decorative topping while the shoots are still opening out.

ABOVE: Hyacinths look wonderful planted one to a pot, then arranged in pairs or larger groups.

RIGHT: Hyacinths are quite happy without compost as long as their roots are kept in water. Set them in glass jars for a light effect that shows off their delicate translucent roots. A ring of autumn leaves tucked around the bulb makes a pretty "collar".

249

TEMPLATES

To enlarge the templates, use either a grid system or a photocopier. For the grid system, trace the template and draw a grid of evenly spaced squares over the tracing. To scale up, draw a larger grid on another piece of paper. Copy the outline on to the second grid by taking each square individually and drawing the relevant part of the outline in the larger square.

ABOVE: Decoupage Eggs

LEFT: Shell Fish Wall Hanging

ABOVE: Mexican Bark Folder

ACKNOWLEDGEMENTS

AUTHOR'S ACKNOWLEDGEMENTS

Let the beauty of nature take the glory for this book as its very essence depends on the wonderful colours, shapes and forms in the world around us. I have had the privilege of working with these, the best materials available and, I hope, perhaps passed on a little of my enthusiasm for all things natural. Thank you to Debbie, whose exquisite photographs have captured this natural beauty, and to her baby Fin, whose delayed arrival meant we could work right into the winter. Thank you, too, to Joanne and Helen who have transformed the material into a brilliant production, and to Nigel for his elegant page design.

The carved pumpkins (pp196-9) were supplied by Mary Maguire and Deborah Schneebeli-Morrell. The driftwood mirror and coathooks (pp134-5, 140-1) were designed by Caroline Cilia, and Deborah Schneebeli-Morrell made the decoupage eggs (pp76-7). Finally, a very big thank you to my family, Richard, Zoë and Faye, for being so patient when the book encroached into the holidays.

PUBLISHER'S ACKNOWLEDGEMENTS

Additional photographs were supplied by Bruce Coleman Limited, p8 (t); by John Shaw, p8 (b); by Sir Jeremy Grayson, p9; by Christer Fredriksson and by the Wildlife and Garden Matters Picture Library, p204, p207 (r), p228 (l) and p229.

SUPPLIERS

UK

CAMERON-SHAW
279 New King's Road
London
SW6 4RD
Tel: 0171 731 8175
Dried arrangements with flair, plus suppliers of dried flowers.

COTTAGE GARDEN ROSES
Woodlands House
Stretton
near Stafford
ST19 9LG
Tel: 01785 840217
Beautiful cottage garden roses and old-fashioned varieties.

DAMASK
Broxholme House
New King's Road
London SW6 4AA
Tel: 0171 731 3553
Linens, cushions, lavender bags.

HAMBLEDEN HERBS
Court Farm
Milverton
Somerset
TA4 1NF
Tel: 01823 410205
Suppliers of medicinal and culinary herbs.

THE HOP SHOP
Castle Farm
Shoreham
Sevenoaks
Kent TN14 7UR
Tel: 01959 523219
Suppliers of good-quality dried hops and other dried flower products.

JEKKA'S HERB FARM
Rose Cottage
Shallards Lane
Alveston
Bristol BS12 2SY
Tel: 01454 418878
Organic herbs and olive trees. Mail order only.

LE GRICE ROSES
Norwich Road
North Walsham
Norfolk NR28 0DR
Tel: 01692 402591
Suppliers of old-fashioned and modern varieties of roses.

NEAL'S YARD REMEDIES
12 Chelsea Farmers' Market
Sydney Street
London SW8 3NS
Tel: 0171 498 1686
Essential oils, dried lavender, roses, rosebuds and other herbs.

NORFOLK LAVENDER
Caley Mill
Heachham
King's Lynn
Norfolk PE31 7JE
Tel: 01485 570384
Growers and suppliers of fresh and dried lavender bunches, loose dried lavender and lavender essential oil.

SOMETHING SPECIAL
263–265 London Road
Mitcham
Surrey CR4 3NH
Tel: 0181 687 0128
Wholesale dried flower and florists' equipment supplier.

THE STENCIL STORE
20/21 Heronsgate Road
Chorleywood
Herts WD3 5BN
Mail order available and stockists all around Britain of a wide variety of stencils plus brushes, paints and sticks.

TUDOR ROSE
Thomas Nurseries
273 Sutton Common Road
Sutton
Surrey SM3 9PZ
Tel: 0181 288 0999
Dried flowers and florists' equipment.

VV ROULEAUX
10 Symons Street
London SW3
Tel: 0171 730 3125
Exquisite ribbons of all kinds.

USA

DODY LYNESS CO.
7336 Berry Hill Dr.
Palos Verdes Peninsula
CA 90274
Tel: (310) 377-7040
Suppliers of pot-pourri, dried
blossoms, herbs, spices, dried
and pressed flowers.

HERB SHOPPE
215 W. Main St.
Greenwood IN 46142
Tel: (317) 889-4395
Suppliers of bulk herbs, pot-
pourri supplies, essential oils,
and other flowers.

GAILANN'S FLORAL CATALOG
821 W. Atlantic St.
Branson MO 65616
Offers a full line of floral
supplies and dried flowers.

JACKSON AND PERKINS
1 Rose Lane
Medford
OR 97501
Tel: (800) USA-ROSE
Suppliers of old-fashioned and
modern varieties of roses.

LÖWE'S OWN ROOT ROSES
6 Sheffield Road
Hashua NH 03062
Tel: (603) 888-2214
Suppliers of old-fashioned and
modern varieties of roses.

SAN FRANCISCO HERB CO.
250 14th St.
San Francisco CA 94103
Offers a full line of herbs and
dried flowers.

TOM THUMB WORKSHOPS
PO Box 357
Mappsville VA 32407
Tel: (804) 824-3507
Suppliers of dried flowers,
ribbons and floral items.

VAL'S NATURALS
PO Box 832
Kathleen
FL 33849
Tel: (813) 858-8991
Suppliers of dried flowers and
pot-pourri ingredients.

AUSTRALIA

BRIDESTOWE ESTATE PTY LTD
RSD 1597
Nabowla
Tas 7254
Tel: (003) 528 182
Lavender farm, retail outlet
stocking oils, dried flowers and
gift lines.

BRUNDRETT & SONS (ROSES)
PTY LTD
Brundrett Road
Narre Warren North
Vic 3804
Tel: (03) 9596 8742
Rose growers and nursery.

HEDGEROW FLOWERS
177 King William Road
Hyde Park, SA 5061
(08) 373 4499
Suppliers of fine-quality roses
and other garden flowers.

HERBS OF GOLD PTY
Unit 5, 102 Bath Road
Krrawee, NSW 2232
Suppliers of medicinal and
culinary herbs.

SOUTHERN LIGHTS HERBS
PO Box 227
Maldon
Vic 3463
Medicinal and culinary herbs.

YUULONG LAVENDER ESTATE
Yendon Rd, Mt Egerton,
Vic 3352
Tel: (053) 689 435
Lavender grower, plant sales
(fresh and dried), lavender
products (craft and cosmetic).

*I*NDEX

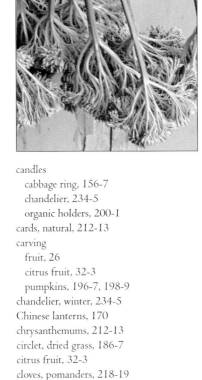